Pengu

Living with
Crazy
Buttocks

Kaz Cooke is the author of *Living with Crazy Buttocks*. She
has two. Impossibly rich and interesting, Kaz divides her
time between martinis, wisecracks and the sort of
throaty chuckle that drives grown men out of their
minds. She wears nothing but whisper-thin satin gowns
in the penthouse of an architecturally significant New
York City skyscraper, which she shares with a winsome
schnauzer and William Powell. It is approximately 1934.

www.kazcooke.com

For Joan Hack

Living with
Crazy
Buttocks

Kaz Cooke

PENGUIN BOOKS

Penguin Books Australia Ltd
487 Maroondah Highway, PO Box 257
Ringwood, Victoria 3134, Australia
Penguin Books Ltd
Harmondsworth, Middlesex, England
Penguin Putnam Inc.
375 Hudson Street, New York, New York 10014, USA
Penguin Books Canada Limited
10 Alcorn Avenue, Toronto, Ontario, Canada M4V 3B2
Penguin Books (N.Z.) Ltd
Cnr Rosedale and Airborne Roads, Albany, Auckland, New Zealand
Penguin Books (South Africa) (Pty) Ltd
5 Watkins Street, Denver Ext 4, 2094, South Africa
Penguin Books India (P) Ltd
11, Community Centre, Panchsheel Park, New Delhi 110 017, India

First published by Penguin Books Australia Ltd 2001

3 5 7 9 10 8 6 4 2

Designed by Nikki Townsend, Penguin Design Studio
Front cover photograph courtesy of photolibrary.com; digital imaging by Paul Fenton
Author's photograph, courtesy of Fox FM, by James Penlidis
Typeset in Weiss by Post Pre-press Group, Brisbane
Printed and bound in Australia by Australian Print Group, Maryborough, Victoria

National Library of Australia
Cataloguing-in-Publication data:

Cooke, Kaz, 1962–.
Living with crazy buttocks.

ISBN 0 14 029723 5.

1. Australian wit and humor. 2. Australia – Anecdotes. I. Title.

A824.3

www.penguin.com.au

Contents

A note to the reader

Several items in this book were written as columns for *The Sydney Morning Herald* and *The Age* newspapers. I would like to thank editors Susan Johnson, Amanda Wilson, Shane Green and John Sharpe; sub-editors Brian Curran (that's his headline on page 312), Fiona McGill (that's hers on page 320), David McMahon and Moira O'Brien-Malone; and the obliging staff of *The Age* editorial library.

The other pieces in this book were heard on radio, mostly on *Foxy Ladies* – a program featuring Judith Lucy and me – which used to be broadcast on Sunday mornings by the Austereo network. Only my scripts for our thrilling radio serial *Casino!* are collected here; none of them reveal that *Casino!* was all Judith's idea and that she wrote many episodes that made people laugh until they were quite ill. The relentless use of only my own material herein gives no clue to the tireless comedic skills, hard work, fine scriptwriting, hilarious delivery and fierce friendship of the incandescently beautiful Miss Lucy. But frankly, enough about her.

At least one of the radio pieces was heard on the Martin/Molloy radio programme. I thank Mr Mick Molloy and Mr Tony Martin for this and many other such opportunities for hijinks. I would like to thank sound suprema Vicki Marr for recording and editing many broadcasts; and the other main voices of *Casino!* – Judith Lucy (damn), Colin Batrouney and Tony Martin.

Get down and get funky
until the all clear

Just in case you ever need to wrestle a crocodile, jump from a revving motorcycle into a moving car or deliver a baby in a taxi, *The Worst-case Scenario Survival Handbook* has been published, in a handy wipe-down laminated cover.

Authors Joshua Piven and David Borgenicht have consulted experts in many fields from identifying bombs to hot-wiring a car to taking a punch. I hope they don't mind me borrowing some of their handy hints to apply to other situations. Some of their suggestions can be just as helpful in everyday life as they are when you need to take on a mountain lion, ram a car or land a plane.

Getting the sack from a company executive
- Avoid talking and smoking.
- Cover the eyes.
- Hit back with an uppercut.
- Do not try to get a closer look, prod it or try to kill it.
- On your way out, give the door several well-placed kicks at the point where the lock is mounted.
- Take the shortest route to firmer ground, moving slowly.

'GET INTO THE LifE Raft, AND TAKE ALL THE SuppLies You caN CarRy'

- Wash the bite with soap and water as soon as you can.
- Wait for your attacker to make a mistake.

Being caught by a ticket inspector when you have no money

- Do not jump into a swimming pool or other body of water: they are likely to be waiting for you when you surface.
- If no shelter is available, run through bushes or high weeds.
- If a safe haven is not available, remove your shirt, hat or another article of clothing.
- Get indoors as fast as you can.

Looking for a new job

- Make your presence known by talking loudly, clapping, singing or occasionally calling out. (Some people prefer to wear bells.)
- Try to make yourself appear bigger by opening your coat wide.

Your plane has been put into a holding pattern above Sydney Airport again

- If the plane has only one set of controls, push, pull, carry or drag the pilot out of the pilot's seat.
- Put on the radio headset (if there is one).
- Jam on the gas.
- Get out.

A stockbroker has asked you to a swimming party

- Do not enter the water if you are bleeding from an open wound.
- Try not to wear any shiny jewellery.
- Always stay in groups.

A person who you thought was your friend has been talking behind your back

- Do not slap its behind to make it cry.
- Clench your jaw.
- Squeeze your feet together.
- Take [a] razorblade or knife and make a half-inch horizontal incision.

A sleazy boss puts the hard word on
- Wear a high-quality helmet and a leather jacket plus leather pants and boots.
- Keep your body completely vertical. Clench your backside and protect your crotch.
- Roll when you hit the ground.
- As soon as you hit the water, open a window.

You have been given a dud birthday present
- Be suspicious of packages wrapped in string – modern packaging materials have eliminated the need for twine or string.
- Call the bomb squad.

You get stuck in a room with senior Liberal politician Peter Reith
- Do not expect firefighters, police or paramedics to be able to help you immediately. They may not be available.
- Three shots from a gun is a recognised distress signal.
- Do not panic, especially if people know where you are and when you are scheduled to return.
- If a car or plane is passing, or if you see other people off in the distance, try to signal to them: use newspaper or aluminium foil weighed down with rocks to make a large triangle, the international distress symbol. An X means you are unable to proceed.

- Get in the life raft and take whatever supplies you can carry.

Your country is a democracy but both major parties are full of dunderheads who can't get health and education right
- Stay bent slightly forward, leaning into the wind.
- Wait for help.
- Fight back if you are attacked.

It's the anniversary of a bad break-up
- Find food.

Joshua Piven and David Borgenicht, *The Worst-case Scenario Survival Handbook*, Chronicle Books, 1999. Used with the permission of the authors and publisher.

A wool boob tube and
a blue carnation

News just in says fashions in gene-altered crops are going gangbusters! It's new! It's fab! It's imperative! Why, they've already invented a blue carnation! And a carnation with a longer vase life! (Look out! I've wee-ed myself!)

Most people under 93 would rather a carnation with no vase life at all. It is not the unblueness of carnations that has seen sales fall: it's just that they're about as fashionable as the name Ethel. Still, press on, science! We can use up the blue carnies by sending them to the infirm who are perhaps suffering from uncontrollable anal leakage, a side effect of that new 'no fat' oil.

Speaking of fashion (shut up), you'll recall last year's fabulous look of a cardigan open down the front but tied together under the bosoms? Celebrities crowd magazine covers dressed only in a bra and an open cardie, sometimes with the sleeves playfully pulled down off the shoulders – ha, ha! (Anybody on the street looking like this has, of course, forgotten their medication, but on a celebrity – phwoarrr!)

What will replace this simply darling look? May I suggest

a squiz at a photo in *Cleo's* '60 Must-have Fashion Looks' (one of which is lingerie with fluffy bunny ears), showing a model wearing a boob tube and a furry hat with earflaps. 'Yes, but what about the arms?' I hear you shriek piteously. 'Oh God, HELP us! What shall we do with our ARMS?'

I have two words for you. These are the words whispered by the fashionable people just as they're being photographed next to someone who's always getting their picture in the paper. Two words. Just. Sleeves. Not attached to anything, just woolly tubes. The kind of thing you could get out of Nanna's knitting basket before she sews a jumper together.

Time Out New York magazine recently shared with us some other variations on the cardie that designers have come up with. The 'shrug' is a cardie with just two sleeves and enough back to provide a bridge between them. And

'Clare Braydon takes her scissors to vintage mohair sweaters to make her cute cut-off tops.' Miss Braydon has cut into a vintage mohair sweater with such fervid concentration that only a neckband and some shoulder covering remain. Hairy epaulets on a choker – divine! The offcuts are not wasted. Lordy, no. They're turned into wristlets – say for when you're wearing a bikini but 5 centimetres of skin above your hands are a tad chilly – and armlets, also known as 'arm warmers'.

The fashion expert explains this 'just sleeves' concept quite perfectly so that practically anyone could understand it: 'Arm warmers . . . are like leg warmers *for your arms.*' (My emphasis.) There's also 'a variation on the poncho', a giant boob tube you put your arms down into as well. This leaves you looking a bit like a rolled-up carpet with shoes on, stuck in an unstaffed elevator going up, down, up, and repeating over and over, 'I'm trapped in a variation of the poncho. But I am funky.'

Another designer has invented a garment (garment! I LOVE it!) that is simply a balaclava attached to some sleeves. (In case the top half of you is snow skiing and the bottom half is in Cape York in January.) And Miki Mialy has invented a woollen boob tube with pockets, each conveniently located over a nipple and roomy enough for half a bus ticket or a crushed mosquito. After all those years of clamouring, finally a designer who's listening to women!

Miki's boob tube has that grey, hand-knitted look: I'd bet it's adapted from one of those old pattern books in which

Whitey Brylcreem Man, wearing a knitted vest featuring contrasting pocket flaps and leathery buttons, gestures with his pipe at an unseen architectural feature, or perhaps a member of the carp family, and fondles with his free hand, in a manly way, the shoulder of the cheerful brute next to him, who sports a poop-brown Aran heart-breaker with double-purl detailing on the waistband, as he sniffs . . . Fancy that! It's a blue carnation.

Writing for profit:

a word from the wise

Writing Magazine, as the cover says, is Essential Reading for *All* Writers, and The Voice of Writing: it suggests its readers should Write Articles that Sell. This is a bonus as I am well past the thrill of Writing Articles that Make the Editor Go All Squinty and Tell You to Get Right the Hell Out.

Mary Brown's 'Advice to Complete Beginners' says one of her favourite ways of catching the editor's eye is to 'present the information in the form of the A–Z, say . . . an A–Z of Christmas customs or an A–Z of rockery plants'. Unfortunately I have already flogged the A–Z of Christmas customs. And if I am any judge of character it would be easier to catch my editor's eye by ockie-strapping myself to his desk in a battery-operated chartreuse bodysuit than dealing in any sense with rockery plants.

Or, Mary suggests, you should pose yourself questions in an article such as 'What is Feng Shui?', followed by 'How can I use Feng Shui in the bedroom?' May I add that the unexpected can work well, such as answering those questions thusly: 'Bolloxed if I know' and 'On yer bike.'

LANCE'S ESCAPE

Jean Saunders takes up this twist-in-the-tail theme by advising that twins as a surprise ending to the mystery story has been overdone. She suggests letting everyone know about the twins and then 'producing a triplet protagonist at the very end'! Brilliant. (Of course, eventually we may have to move on to quintuplets.)

Back to Mary, who is still chocker with ideas: 'You could get six friends to try a certain regime or beauty plan for a week and then write a report on the results.' I say, pals, why not starve yourselves for a week or put lard on your bosoms so I can sell an article? Thought not.

'Lastly,' explains Mary, 'perhaps you could do one of those "day in the life of . . ." features . . . Interview your local vicar or the Master of Foxhounds, or a homeless person. Be sure to provide at least one good photograph.' (If you have a photograph of something that the Master of

Foxhounds is doing to the vicar that was shot by a homeless person, please give this organ a tingle.)

There's an ad in the magazine for a book called *How to Become a Freelance Journalist* by James Slater. In my own experience this is achieved quite simply by joining an independent newspaper, which will have its funding cut off quicksticks and then you don't have a job, so you are a freelance journalist. How Mr Slater is going to stretch that over more than a chapter or two is a mystery. He must be really good at adjectives.

There's another book advertised called *Lights and Sirens* by James and Lois Cowan, a writers' guide to fifteen different emergency services in the USA. (You wouldn't want to write about a paramedic coming in with a hot-pink cardigan, kitten-heeled sling-backs and a nozzle-reversed awhimaway trolley unless that was standard issue.) The book also details medical procedures and drugs used in certain circumstances, such as precisely when everyone is to yell 'Stat!' or say 'Nurse Hathaway, would you step outside so I can give you a soulful look and a tongue kiss right near the admissions desk.'

There is an article on a company that has captured 75 per cent of the cross-stitching magazine market in Britain and then boldly produced *Cake Decoration* magazine, which is 'keen to feature more people who have made cakes for celebrities'. If you fancy trying a ginger fluff sponge for Courtney Love, I've got its address.

Margaret Geraghty has something to say on the subject

of plausible cliffhangers. She disparages a writer who put his hero, Lance O'Neill, in 'a deep, straight-sided pit with knives jutting out of it', and then began the next chapter, 'With a mighty leap, Lance sprang out of the pit.' All I ask is to know whether Lance could be described as wearing a loincloth. Also, is Lance acquainted with the oeuvre of Barbra Streisand? Or on the other hand give me his telephone number immediately.

Next week: our crack at the romance story.

Suddenly, a romance story

for our times

As promised, here is our romance story inspired by *Writing Magazine*.

Shazza flicked back her honey-blonde fringe, which was making it difficult to see the line. If there was any sticky tape left at home she'd have to give it a trim tonight. The production line had suddenly slowed – perhaps someone had lost a finger further up the line – and she had more time to de-beak the poultry as it whizzed past.

Her green eyes flashing, Shazza, who had quite a trim, size 16 figure and was wearing a yellow nylon shift, with a Peter Pan collar, under her regulation plastic coat, and knee-high rubber boots, dreamed of the day when she would be able to get away from the plant, and sleazy Mr Hornbag. Suddenly, she raised a rubber-gloved hand to her peachy cheek, her grey eyes sombre in the fluorescent light and the haze caused by dust and chemicals.

Suddenly, her carbon-lashed blue eyes lifted as the siren for lunch sounded. Finally, she'd be able to get to the Ladies'. They docked your pay or fired you if you left the

THE MOB FROM DISPATCH

line when it was moving. If Mr Hornbag detected any birds with beaks downwind, there'd be hell to pay. Shazza pulled off her hairnet and made for the canteen.

Bent over her rissoles, Shazza didn't hear Mr Hornbag come up behind her until he suddenly had his hand on her shoulder. Suddenly, he was hurled away in a swirl of velveteen and gold-edged cloakery, and a deep voice like John Laws's, only not as expensive, stilled the chatter of the canteen.

'By God's teeth, I'll have you flayed for that!' said the stranger, who was built like a double-freezer and was wearing tights, puffy dacks and a gigantic hat with curly tail-feather bits. He had flashing dark eyes, a troubled brow and a couple of Explorer socks down the front of his jocks. His thighs were very powerful and his mouth was cruel and sardonic, although Shazza felt sure he was the type to tip waitresses and be nice to littlies.

'You're not from round here, are ya?' She bit back her query suddenly.

'You're sacked!' spluttered Mr Hornbag suddenly, lying on the floor in a pool of polyester.

'Who's ya supervisor?'

'Ha ha,' laughed the stranger in a hard way. 'I am Prince Grigor Cruelto of the Prussian noblery-type persons and thither come my suzerains with their scullions yonder.' He pointed to most of the mob from Dispatch, who were suddenly looking a bit confused.

'Wouldst ye possess yourself of this maid's treasure?' he demanded. 'Yea, I see it in your eyes, you swine of Satan's devil-nipple. Begone afore thee is meat to my javelin.'

Shazza bit her lip and stared down at her rubber boots, suddenly. She was going to be docked for sure. Prince Grigor's voice suddenly softened as he sat next to her on a moulded plastic chair and helped her open the sachet of tomato sauce.

'They're a bastard, aren't they,' she said suddenly, 'specially if you've done all ya fingernails on beaks.'

Prince Grigor ran his chainmail-gloved finger suddenly down her cheekbone as her hazel eyes took in his tender yet steely gaze.

Suddenly, there was a misunderstanding. Probably because of something Kyandra from Stock said, Prince Grigor got hold of the wrong end of the stick and thought

Shazza was a slag. Which, as Shazza pointed out to Marge from Accounts, was bloody unfair. She had been a slag for a while because she'd thought it was compulsory, but since March she'd realised she didn't have to be a slag even if they reckoned she was one and it was an enormous bloody relief, to tell you the truth.

She lifted her yellow, cat-like eyes filled with tears to see Kyandra offering Prince Grigor some of her Fanta and a dim sim. Suddenly, the siren went. Shazza stood up, suddenly tired, wondering if she was about to get her period. Suddenly, Prince Grigor appeared at her side.

'Here's a letter recommending you to a decent bloke who runs a hot-bread shop that's looking for staff down the mall. You get an hour off for lunch and you can sit down if there's no customers.'

'Thanks,' said Shazza, suddenly red eyed. 'You're a real Prince.'

Men of allure: a force
to be reckoned with

We present our latest report in this lyrical point-form essay entitled 'Compare and Contrast the Magazines *Men of Allure* (Undated) and a Recent Edition of *Army*'.

1   *Men of Allure* makes one laugh out loud when looking at the front cover. Opening the magazine and looking at anything in there will have you howling on the carpet, calling for towels.

2   The cover boasts a man with a ludicrous expression so come-hitherish as to be run-for-the-hills-erish, and cover lines such as 'What Cheryl Ladd Really Eats', 'The World's Most Sensational Men' and 'Celebrity Nude! Pop Star Marilyn'. (Someone has left the page numbers off the contents list.) One of the slightly clad models in the mag is called Hawkin Stravinsky. There is also a picture story over several pages about 'ambitious young criminal lawyer Bo Ventura' who, as it happens, likes nothing more than showing anybody his willy.

3   Favourite *Men of Allure* picture caption: '"What's your name?" you ask, getting even closer. "Mark," he answers.' (Brainy, huh?) Second-favourite picture caption: 'The nude body is the subject of many works of art, says the former art history student [Antoine], here doing his impression of Michelangelo's *David*.' (Let's see him have a crack at the *Venus de Milo*, I say.)

4   *Men of Allure* reports that Cheryl Ladd has dessert, and this is a direct quote, 'once a year'. *Army* magazine does not mention Cheryl Ladd.

5   Favourite picture caption from *Army* magazine: 'Crews from 3/9LH (SAMR) study a mud model as part of 12/40RTR's counter-penetration plan.' This accompanies a photo of some blokes standing around while another bloke draws on the ground with a stick. (This differs markedly from the photos in *Men of Allure* in that the *Army* people seem to actually know what they're doing, rather than just standing around with their scrotums out. I feel this augurs quite well for the defence of our land.) Second-favourite photo caption: 'As with the Sykes-Fairbairn dagger, a skull-crusher pommel graces the Tanto.'

6   Point of contrast: an *Army* feature on the school of artillery is rather long on hydraulics and the 105-millimetre howitzer and fairly short on himbos who see no reason to keep their dacks on and who seem to have had their names made up by casting agents who were hallucinating pretty badly.

7   Point of similarity: each magazine explores the theme of chaps in the jungle. See for yourself how the skilful use of emphasis differentiates between the two. *Men of Allure* features a naked man in a headband frotting around some palm trees with the caption: 'You cheered Rambo. You adored Commando. But you couldn't be stranded in the jungle with a better companion than Mark Allan.' (Especially if you enjoy men who waggle their 'nads in the fernery.)

8   Personally, if I had to be stranded in the jungle, I would probably rather be with Trooper Charles

McGregor Shaw, a student of a combat survival training course run by Townsville RAAF base. Although he is grubby and sweaty and fairly insane looking in his *Army* photo, this is because he had been without much to eat or a wash for three days and had been getting around in the mud avoiding pretendy enemy patrols out looking for him. The trooper is also a good conversationalist: '"I thought the sea phase would be a little easier but sitting in a raft with four other people hanging over the side spewing, and one guy on lookout spewing as well, was quite bad."'

9   *Army* has a photo of another soldier on the survival course holding up a rat skin (the rest was stewed), which is quite a marked contrast to 'Mark' in *Men of Allure*, who looks like a mouse would cause him to stand on a chair and simply scream the house down.

10 In conclusion, I would like to say that *Men of Allure* has surprisingly little in common with *Army* magazine. There are a lot of blokes in both of them, but if it comes to repelling hostile armed predators I would rather rely on the dedicated men and women of our defence forces than, say, Bo Ventura and Hawkin Stravinsky. It's nothing personal. I just think they're kind of underdressed.

Pass on the plutonium,

Pongo old chap

'A firm looking at building a high-level nuclear waste dump in outback Australia says it will not go ahead with the proposal if Australians do not want the dump.'

— *The Age*, 6 March 1999

Charmed, we're sure.

Dr Charles McCombie, the head honcho of Pangea Resources (I love the way it's called a 'firm', as if they all sit about in pinstripes and bowler hats asking Pongo to pass the Earl Grey), says let's dig a dirty great hole in Australia and ship in some highly radioactive wastes: 'We think it's the . . . best thing to do with the 2000 tonnes of highly enriched uranium lying around the world, not being looked after and sought by terrorists with millions of dollars to spend.'

(Please. If there are terrorists wandering around wanting to spend millions, they need only look at the fashion pages of the newspapers' weekend magazines.)

The Australian desert regions of Western Australia and

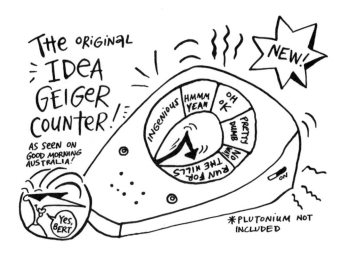

South Australia look good to Pangea because there's not as much ground water as in a rainforest, there's a 'low population' ('Yoo-hoo! Terra nullius? Anybody home?'), earthquakes are unlikely, and it's low-sloping topography. Several bits have already been suggested by Pangea as great spots to park something so ghastly it makes the Old Testament Devil look like Tinkerbell after four chardonnays.

One of the bits belongs to the Arabunna people of South Australia, some of whom still wish to drink from springs and eat bush tucker in the area. The Kupa Piti Kunga Tjuta women's group, based in Coober Pedy, opposes the dump. As would any sensible citizen who isn't into trepanning (that's drilling holes in your own skull).

An Internet search yielded some of Dr McCombie's thoughts from papers such as the imaginatively entitled 'Multinational Repositories: A Win–Win Disposal Strategy'.

He co-authored this: 'The increased importance of engineered barriers is in part a reaction to the increasing awareness of the difficulties in characterising complex geologic systems with the resolution and the accuracy required for repository analysis.' I'm not sure what this means exactly but if I were him I'd just say, 'Rats. We were kind of hoping we could just bury this crap in Nevada and go play tennis, but how can we predict what those damned rocks'll do eventually?'

Transporting the nuclear waste here will be simple. I'm thinking rubber dinghies to the coast, and then bike couriers can follow the route of the Olympic flame, with plutonium bricks in their saddlebags. Security will be provided by remote-controlled dingoes with AK47s.

Dr McCombie told a conference on dumping, organised by conservation groups in Adelaide last week, that he has homes in Aberdeen, Scotland and Switzerland but is presently based in Perth. He's also co-authored this: 'Whether through erosion or uplift, a successful site must have no mechanisms capable of directly exposing wastes at the ground surface over periods of up to a million or more years.' Doc, you may as well take your playlunch and go awa' home tae Innesbruck. This is the official position of just about every Australian on nuclear waste dumps here: not on your nellie.

Pangea insists that a nuclear tip would enhance Australia's international standing, contribute to world peace, solve the problem of multiple dangerous dumps worldwide and earn us lots of money. (What's the GST on harbouring the most endlessly poisonous fanatic-magnet in the known universe?)

Pangea is 70 per cent owned by the British Nuclear Fuels company, which owns the notorious Sellafield nuclear power plant. Recently the company's chief executive officer fell on his letter opener after revelations of data falsification at the plant. According to the company website, the hobbies of the new CEO are skiing, fell-walking and golf, not widely enjoyed in Australian deserts.

'It's the latest round in a sorry saga of nuclear colonialism,' Dave Sweeney from the Australian Conservation Foundation said this week, after I told him he wasn't allowed to say 'anathema'. 'The idea of turning part of Australia into a foreign-controlled nuclear sacrifice zone is not on, now or in the future.'

On the British Nuclear Fuels website, 'Where Science Never Sleeps', an adorable cartoon atom in wee boots gestures with white gloves and says, 'Hello, I'm the mighty atom . . . there's a BNFL site near you.' No there isn't. And that's very fine by us.

Battle of the sexes

HOST: Welcome back to *Battle of the Sexes*. Craig – what is a uterus?

CRAIG: It's a very tough muscular organ of the female pelvis, mate, about the size of a small pear, controlled by a muscle known as myometrium and lined with cell layers called endometrium. The . . .

HOST: No, mate, we were looking for 'something to do with a crankshaft'. Let's see if the ladies can pull one off. Amanda: name one famous car driver.

AMANDA: Sarah Jessica Parker?

Ivy's gardening tips

Hello, it's Ivy here with gardening tips for January.

1   Mulch the garden thoroughly. This is done by

putting on a nice pair of stiletto shoes and doing the boogie-woogie surfer stomp on your garden beds. If necessary, you can poke them with a stick, and I find that goes for people as well.

2   Look out for aphids on the roses. If you see any, lay down some suppressive fire with a semi-automatic rifle until you can get your hands on some industrial chemicals and spray the buggers into the middle of next week. It will cause birth defects, but it does liquify the entrails of aphids and that's the main thing.

I've been spraying for years and it hasn't done me the slightest bit of cinnamon tea cake and a cuppa tea, thanks love.

And don't forget to widdle on the lemon tree! Ta-ta for now.

Hoist-it ads

[*harp music*]

THREE GIRLY VOICES [*singing*]:   Hoist-it Corsetry and Corrections. Paris, New York and Burnie!

WOMAN: A full bust needs a bra that gives good support. Here at Hoist-it, we recommend the pretty Block and Tackle style, in Bri-nylon. And remember, ladies: the natural look may be cheap – but who wants to look cheap?

MAN: You've seen push-up Wonderbras for women.
You've seen those bosoms hoisted shoulder high and
waved in the breeze. Imagine something that could
do the same for your scrotum. Yes, Wonderpants for
men. A size 10 Explorer sock sewn into the Y-front of
every pair. Make them wonder – with Wonderpants.

Boinin' oiges

My sexual fantasy is that a tall, dark, handsome stranger
with big hands comes around to my place in a cowboy hat,
speaks to me in a Scottish accent, plays a bit of percussion,
does the dishes, vacuums, waters the garden, tidies my
underpants drawer, makes my lunch, has a chat about current events and goes home . . .

I just read a book called *Burning Urges* by News Limited
columnist Ruth Ostrow, in which she has collected the sexual fantasies of Australians who wrote to her describing
them. I thought it might be a bit raunchy, but in fact it was
mostly very puzzling.

One woman was very excited by the idea of a man
who approached her in the Safeway's car park, produced
a street directory and asked for directions. Frankly I
would have said, 'What do you need me for, sunshine?
You've got a street directory.'

A 41-year-old married man fantasised about being tied

up in a rubber raincoat and a balaclava. He's probably not from southern Tasmania.

I was a little startled to learn that some people are getting ideas from watching SBS movies. One woman described a scene she likes to copy in which a man stands in the kitchen while a woman gets out a bowl of chocolate mousse and sits in it. That, to my mind, isn't sexy – that's a criminal waste of chocolate mousse.

And a surprising number of ordinary suburban folk wanted a threesome or group sex. And I know I'm sounding like Mrs Vanilla, but I would just be too nervous. I can't remember people's names at the best of times let alone when we're all in the nuddy playing Twister in a vat of custard.

How to declutter your colon

Just when you think the New Age movement has exhausted all avenues of fact-shirking nonsense, rejoice! For there will always be people having a bit of a chat out of their rectum.

While researching my *Little Book of Dumb Feng Shui* (pronounced 'dum fung shway'), I encountered the book *Clear Your Clutter with Feng Shui* by Karen Kingston. Specifically, I'm afraid, the section entitled 'The Ideal Bowel Movement'.

Ms Kingston, a Pom who can send you Balinese space-clearing bells, is a big fan of colon cleansing, claiming that 'Many herbalists advocate colon cleansing as the cure for 90 per cent of all diseases.' So it is quite obvious that Ms Kingston either knows one or two barkingly insane herbalists, or is professor of chemistry at the University of Loobyloo Falala Land.

Anyway, I am just being a cynical old piece of negative space really, because Ms Kingston explains: 'If the colon is clogged, it affects everything you do. If you need any more convincing, Dr Richard Anderson tells of a very revealing

experiment . . .' This involves some Nobel prize winner called Alexis Carrel who 'kept animal tissues alive indefinitely' by feeding them and washing away excretions. 'He kept a chicken heart alive for 29 years until someone failed to cleanse its excretions.' Jeez, I'm convinced. What of is another matter.

Dr Carrel, it should be pointed out, was actually doing something useful in the way of wound research, whereas Dr Anderson's self-published book *Cleanse and Purify Thyself* is available by mail order from Healthforce Regeneration Systems in Santa Fe, whose website features humungously disconcerting photographs of 30-centimetre-long poo (do not go there), the like of which apparently came out of Dr Anderson after he had been in the desert eating only herbs. The website records he was 'utterly amazed'. Aren't we all, sunshine.

Anyway, back in the real world or, oops, perhaps not, Ms Kingston goes on: 'I believe the dumbest thing a person can do when they are seriously ill is to eat anything at all.' I agree totally, and it's probably better if they cut their legs off as well. Damned limbs, cluttering up the joint.

She also reports that breast cancer in developing countries may be caused by the introduction of bras, and that underwire bras in particular attract harmful electromagnetic fields from computers and other electrical appliances into delicate breast tissue, 'contributing to the likelihood of breast cancer'.

I couldn't agree more that a spring clean of the odd cupboard can be more useful than poking off your ears with a toasting fork. But this war on clutter as philosophy has gorn too far. In some cases right back to the Middle Ages.

According to Ms Kingston, 'It is best not to do space clearing if you are pregnant, menstruating or have an open wound.' You should BURN IN HELL before you clean up your coffee table while having a period, YOU VILE GODLESS UNCLEAN BRIDE OF SATAN. (And if you're suffering from the black plague, opening a vein is a great home remedy.)

Also, while decluttering, 'Remove jewellery and other metallic objects from your person.' Possibly because, as well as attracting those electromagnetic vicious thingie vibes, you could accidentally start receiving some easy-listening stations from Uranus.

'Clap in corners to disperse static energy. Then wash

your hands in running water (very important to remember to do this),' Ms Kingston says. She also tells the story of a woman who 'noticed that the prosperity corner of her bedroom was very empty'. So she filled it with flowers and that very night her husband gave her 'a thousand pounds' to spend on anything she pleased!

Ms Kingston points out that people who have cluttered homes are often overweight. Evidence? Oh, get out.

It is mentioned, oh, about 676,890,000 times in the book that Ms Kingston lives in Bali. One can only imagine that one day she noticed that the bullshit corner of her home was empty. So she filled it with copies of *Clear Your Clutter with Feng Shui*, and people bought the book, and she decided to go where it's cheaper to get servants to clear up your clutter.

Admittedly I don't know this for a fact. I'm intuiting it through electromagnetic waves coming from my computer.

Karen Kingston, *Clear Your Clutter with Feng Shui*, Broadway Books, 1991.

How long is a piece of string theory?

Oh, now they berloody tell us. Twelve years of asking, 'What good will maths do us in real life?', and being told one day we might need to find out how high a barn is if its shadow was at an angle of an isosceles algorithm (shut up), and NOW a research institute has posted a $12 million prize if you can solve seven maths problems.

That's $1.76 million per problem, according to the papers. I haven't checked. I haven't checked because I can't do maths. I've even forgotten my times tables. If you offered me $3.4 million for knowing 8 times 9, I honestly would have to go home and have a sardine sandwich. Because when I went to school maths was so cruelly tedious it sent children into stunned, scary silences, and they had to be sent to the mountains with warm bonnets on.

Now, of course, maths classes are wildly exciting and involve aerial work and electric shocks. Also, after about 20,000 and pi-squared generations, it has finally sunk in that, yes, students need maths and can regularly thrill to the singular pleasure of knowing they are absolutely, unutterably correct.

But 2 plus 2, I'm very much afraid, is incapable of being any more interesting than four. As far as I'm concerned, this is the whole ludicrous problem with maths, and the reason why I couldn't do it: you can't just have a decent stab at it. Take this competition, for instance: for each problem there is only one specific right answer. (So how will they know when a genius has got it right? I plan to send a very vehement letter saying, '6.7! Hurrah for me!' It's worth a go.)

Questions are more interesting when they have several possible answers, such as 'A margarita and some peanuts – no wait, a glass of stout. Or, in some cases, simply remove your trousers.' Or, as one mouldy textbook at the back of the third drawer down puts it, 'A confectioner purchases, in bulk, three assortments of chocolate – hard centres (H);

soft centres (S); and ruffles (R). He mixes them in various proportions and retails them in half-kilogram packets under three brand names: King (K), Pacific (P) and New England (N). The proportions are shown in the following matrix:

	H	S	R
K	0.4	0.3	0.3
P	0.6	0	0.4
N	0.5	0.5	0

The retail prices per packet are King 69c, Pacific 68c and New England 65c. Determine the price per half kilogram of each assortment.'

I rather think I shan't. Surely the pertinent questions here are: how pissed off would you be if you bought a packet of Pacific choccies and found out there were no (zero) (0.0) soft centres? What the blithering buggery blazes is a ruffle? And why conceal that information from the bargain-hunting purchaser of a packet of the zingingly titled New England chocolates? Also, were chocolates really that cheap when I was at school? If so, why am I fatter now? Another daunting (or exciting) thing about maths is that there are so many kinds (PLEASE. Don't START me with Binomial Hypergeometric Distributions): complex numbers (why not simplify them a bit?); algebra; geometry; calculus; matrices; theoretical string theory physics; and statistics. (These are great. You'll need to understand these to decipher newspaper articles that say stuff like: if you're an educated woman with a job, your children are more likely to be thick as planks because you're a selfish cow. Also, men should not bother being around when their kids are small because on average the kids hardly notice, but should turn up again when they are teenagers because by then the kids have probably started noticing.) It's amazing what they can deduce by asking the right questions.

For example, find the cartesian equation of the curves whose parametric equations are: $x = t$, $y = t^2$, t (funny squiggly weird symbol I don't have on my keyboard) R. And I think you'll find the answer is very definitely: depends. Can I have the money now?

The maths is from J. B. Fitzpatrick and P. L. Galbraith, *Pure Mathematics: Modern Mathematics 6*, Jacaranda, 1981.

Ask me no questions and
I'll fill in the form

The other day a polite university student knocked on the door and asked if he could have 30 minutes of my time. As I was combing the chenille bedspreads and making curtain tassels out of recycled fence posts, I was in. It became clear that this would involve answering questions devised by a frightfully respected polling organisation.

Don't you ever see those poll results and think, 'Who the hell are they asking? Small but opinionated ferrets? Regulars at the One Nation Lobotomy Hostel?' Here was a chance to even the score. The student (I shall call him Gavin. Not because I need to but because it lends an air of mystery, research and truth) settled at the table with a mug of crème de menthe, a digestive biscuit and a Biro.

Obviously, Gavin's goal was to charge through the enormous booklet of questions as quickly as possible, get out of the house, put a few more interviews under his belt, finish his degree and spend the next fifty years (a) paying it off, and (b) being depressed because the government had abolished student unions so he had no support or available services or information during that most vulnerable age

ACCURATE POLLING:

and thought he had tertiary syphilis, whereas in fact it was tinea.

Anyway, this meant the best answers from Gavin's point of view were straightforward and succinct. But when someone asks, 'Who would you vote for if an election were held tomorrow: the Liberal Party–National Party Coalition, the ALP or One Nation?', I would normally say, 'If a One Nation candidate stood in this electorate they'd have less chance than a Pollywaffle of getting a seat in parliament.

'And where are the other choices, such as that nice Natasha woman in the purple jumper? I do like a Democrat who sticks to her principles in a cable knit. Or a nice wee Greens candidate in form-fitting mohair. Being asked to select from the pollster's list is a bit like, say, choosing between the Ku Klux Klan, Genghis Khan and a bunch of canoeing fanciers with ill-matching paddles.'

There was, however, no space on the form for that.

Then I was asked to describe Mr Beazley, Mr Howard and Mr Costello by selecting adjectives from a list. I could choose as many as I liked from stuff like 'trust-worthy', 'weak' and 'intelligent'. Gavin said there was no 'blindingly mediocre'. Or 'casually vicious bastard'. Or even 'a rambunctious liar with a tendency to announce dreadful things while pretending they're wonderful in such an infuriating way it causes an ineluctable wish to sneak up behind and whack him on the back of the head with a rolled-up newspaper.' Not even 'adorable raunchy humanitarian'.

None of the above, then.

'What about "dishonest"?' suggested a passer-by (we have an open-plan living area).

It wasn't on the list. Gavin tried not to look surprised. There was also no space for the nuance, the considered comment or the possibility that Peter Costello and Simon Crean are the same entity in separate bodies, from the tiresome planet of Smirko-gloatypants.

Then we got onto cars. Of the list of car companies in front of me, which went on until approximately just this side of infinity, which ones showed leadership? Eh? Gav was waiting for an answer. I wondered if, say, the manag-ing director of Chrysler wanted me to arm myself and storm Baltimore, would I follow? And if an Audi engineer called looking for volunteers to form a relief brigade to Cuba, would I simply pack the maracas and call a cab?

No, I decided, somewhat tragically, I can't think of a single car company that shows leadership. No wonder the world's going to Helena Handbasket. I had been under the rather antique impression that car companies should perhaps be making cars and decently dealing with their workers and customers. Apparently my priorities are a bit shithouse. Clearly, the car companies are more worried about whether they are showing 'leadership'. Haven't they got better things to do with their time?

I certainly have, so I sent Gavin on his way with a couple of hedgehogs wrapped in greaseproof paper and celebrated by crocheting a Hills Hoist cover out of discarded support hose. It had just been so exhilarating to stand up and be counted.

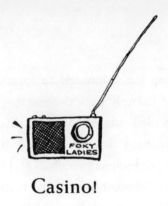

Casino!

Episode one

A searing radio drama for many voices.

[*fade up thrilling theme music*]

ANNOUNCER: *Foxy Ladies* invites you to stay tuned for their splendid radio serial, *Casino!*, sponsored by Hoist-it Corsetry and Corrections. Yes, it's *Casino!* Adventure! Intrigue! Ruin! Starring:

> **Miss Gloria Sarse** as Joan Hack, the washed-up, dried-up old —

JOAN HACK: Hey!

ANNOUNCER: Sorry.

> . . . **Miss Petula Slingback** as Lizzie Goody Good, the airhead socialite with a heart of flummery
> **Humphrey Steamer-Trunk** as John Goody Good, the mysterious African

explorer with a shady past
Dame Margaret Passage as Lady
Chooky Cripps, the rich nympho with
a silver spoon in her cleavage
and introducing –
Errol Vermouth as Dash Trowel, the
manly private dick with a heart. Or
has he?

Don't touch that dial, for it's *Casino!*
[*theme music ends*]

ANNOUNCER: Lizzie Goody Good has just admitted
in the casino's powder room –
LIZZIE GOODY GOOD [*breathlessly*]: I must try to
remember why I have no legs. But first I shall
go and find my husband, John. He makes me
so divinely happy.
[*babble of voices*]
ANNOUNCER: And now we join Joan Hack and Dash
Trowel near the casino car park.
[*sounds of crying children, car doors slamming, muted crying*]
JOAN [*exceedingly sardonically*]: Well, if it isn't Dash Trowel,
private dick. Let's go inside and get a martini.
[*casino noise fades up*]
DASH TROWEL [*very Bogartly*]: Hello, sweetheart. I
always did like a redhead in Glomesh culottes.

JOAN: Actually, that's my cellulite. Call me Joan.

           [*aside*] Hello, Bunty.

DASH: Have you seen a pert little party called Lizzie

           Goody Good?

JOAN [*suspicious*]:   What's your business, gumshoe?

           Here's Lizzie now.

LIZZIE: Hello, Miss Hack, who's your pal?

DASH: Dash Trowel at your service, miss.

LIZZIE: Oh, I'm a *Mrs*, thank God! [*aside*] Have you

           seen John? Perhaps he's in the smirking room.

           He likes smirking.

[*babble of noises*]

LADY CHOOKY CRIPPS [*Lady-Bracknell-meets-cheap-slut*

           tones]:   Hello there, big boy! Care to twirl a

           tassel on a bosom the size of the *Titanic*?

DASH: Lady Chooky Cripps, you look like 300

           pounds of heavenly joy, but I'm the quiet

           type.

LADY CHOOKY: You wouldn't have to *say* anything,

           you silly little man. Why, my fifth husband

           didn't make a squeak until the divorce, and it

           then became clear he was an itinerant Polish

           cleaner who thought he'd been living in a

           Braille version of *Veronica's Closet*. Oh, hello,

           Bunty.

JOAN: Back off, Lady Cripps, this one's mine.

LADY CHOOKY: Suffering servants, Joan! Anyone

           would think you wanted the little squirt all to

yourself! Why, in my day, gels could have a vigorous massacre of hockey together in the afternoon, scarf down a midnight feast with Mildred of the Upper Fourth at midnight and ravish a couple of sailors, before strapping down our busts and invading Corsica. Look out, there goes an under-19 soccer team! I'm orf. Tally-ho!

[*babble of voices*]

ANNOUNCER: Tune in to *Casino!* next week, when you'll hear Dash Trowel say –

DASH: Lizzie, I'm afraid I've got some bad news. The man you think is your husband – barracks for Collingwood.

LIZZIE [*uncontrollable hysterics*] . . .

[*music out*]

Apparently we'd all be much happier in the nuddy

Once upon a time Paul Wilson published *The Little Book of Calm* and it sold approximately 14 gerzillion copies, was a bestseller in England and made me so tense that, as regular readers will recall, I immediately had to write *The Little Book of Stress*.

Mr Wilson's calming suggestions (one thought per tiny page) included ideas such as always wear white, sing Christmas songs and watch fish. As you can well imagine, this made one rigid with a fury only alleviated by a great deal of shouting at the small volume in question.

Anyway, since then Mr Wilson has written *The Little Book of Calm at Work* and, now, *The Little Book of Pleasure*. *The Little Book of Holiday Houses on Five Continents and the Odd 60-foot Yacht* cannot be far behind. Good on him.

But may we dwell for a moment on *The Little Book of Pleasure*? I don't wish to be impertinent, but I believe I can only add to the great tidal whoosh of pleasure for readers if I may help them better grasp some of Mr Wilson's bits. Here's one: **'At least once in your life savour a fresh garden salad, picked before your very eyes, in Provence.'** (All these quotes are fair dinkum.)

'Communicate with somebody without uttering a word'

You'll notice this is a multi-faceted task. It seems easy, but as with many pleasures it is not simple. First, you have to get yourself to Provence, which presumably is somewhere in Scandinavia, or possibly Portugal. You'll be needing travel insurance, long khaki shorts, and maybe a Swiss Army knife, although you could buy one cheaper over there if Provence turns out to be in Switzerland.

Secondly, you will have to locate a vegie patch and then incite a passer-by to pluck you some salad vegetables. Also, it must happen before your very eyes – no turning away or just sitting in a cafe ordering a salad. If you do that, you'll have to follow the waiter through the kitchen and out to a paddock, all the while watching, watching.

Thirdly, no bolting down the salad, and no saying, 'Yeah, it was all right, I s'pose': you have to *savour* it. I realise it seems like we've exhausted the subject but, finally, on no account should you order a Greek salad, or a caesar salad or one of those groovy parmesan and roquette thingies. It must be a garden salad. Right. That's all. Off you go.

'Kiss a friend (or a complete stranger) under a waterfall.' First, find a stranger. No, first, find a waterfall. No, first . . . Oh, bugger it.

'Feel the relief as you sink into a queen-size mattress after a strenuous day on your feet.' Presumably the bed size is important because the heading reads: 'Ease down on a queen.' Oh, baby, fluff my tulle.

'Try standing naked and spread-eagled in a brisk wind, allowing it to caress you in ways that are decidedly natural.' And then try explaining it down at the station.

'Communicate with somebody important (to you) without uttering a word.' It's crucial to get this one right. If you go off making silent gestures at important people (as opposed to people who are important to you), you may well find yourself in serious trouble, like that guy who got arrested for spitting at Jeff Kennett. Ways that you can communicate with a person who is important to you without using words include: kicking them under the table to get them to shut the hell up; making a corkscrew motion with your index finger pointed at your temple to indicate nuttiness; and biting their extremities.

'Make love.' (And if you don't have a partner, just get stuffed.)

'Indulge in the visual sensuousness as you and your

partner sit naked, untouching, and appreciate one another.' (If you're still awake after a minute and a half, you're not parents of small children.)

'What a delight it is', Mr Wilson concludes, 'to suppose there are hundreds of thousands of people – maybe just like you – who are discovering the world is a much more enjoyable place than the evening news would have us believe.'

Well, exactly. The sooner all those refugees suppose themselves over to Provence and just insist someone makes them a garden salad in front of their very eyes, the happier they'll be.

Paul Wilson, *The Little Book of Pleasure*, Penguin Books Australia, 1998. Used with the permission of the author and publisher.

The Pundypants Institute

picks a winner

You know how every election they wheel out people they call pundits? And it's usually some really cranky-lookin' guy called Ferdie Mackerras – I don't know what he does between federal elections, maybe whacks ferrets (I'm just testing the libel laws) – or former senator Graham Richardson, who famous people fondly call Richo. (The rest of this paragraph was lost in transmission.)

I looked up 'pundit' in the dicto and it's Hindi, from the Sanskrit. It means a learned Hindu, one versed in Sanskrit and in the philosophy, religion and jurisprudence (it was a Beatles song) of India. It also means a learned expert or teacher. This week I am punding.

I am going to pund the current election of the Diet Coke Guy (I was alerted to the election by a full-page ad in *Who Weekly* magazine). The elected Diet Coke Guy will have many responsibilities, which mainly will have to do with being a guy and being in a Diet Coke ad. Also, the winner of the competition will get a brand new MGf. I'm not entirely rigid on this point, but I'm pretty sure that's either some kind of flooring material or a Russian jet

fighter aircraft. You can probably get them in ecru. Which is a colour. Or a small continent. But let's get on.

There are six candidates for Diet Coke Guy. They have been photographed standing together, each with a Diet Coke bottle in hand, and if their expressions are anything to go by there's one clenched by each set of undulatory buttocks as well. (You can't actually see any undulating in the photo. I'm pundextrapolating.) The candidates are labelled Guy 01 to Guy 06. Why they need a zero in there is a matter of some conjecture. There's a teeny tiny possibility the campaign has been designed by utter wankers.

Okay, so in this toothy white field of six are two firefighters. Why are they wasting our time? There are two FIREFIGHTERS. (Firefighters, ay. Phwoooaaarrr.) Laydown misère. If there is anything women have more fantasies about than firefighters it's got something to do with equal pay, a family-friendly workplace and/or a moment to themselves. Ha ha ha ha ha ha ha ha. Aaaah dear. What a roarer. (I've got a million of 'em.)

It's always a good idea, however, to cast a pundy eye over the field as there could be what is called a dark horse. This is Sanskrit for an underdog who gallops home approximately three lengths (of Bass Strait) ahead of the rest. Could it be Kristian Spencer, 21, of Gisborne, who sells something unspecified, whose only cooking experience is baked beans and whose best feature is his smile? We here at the Pundypants Institute (just round the corner from the Ponds Institute) think not. Kristian, unfortunately, looks like a kindergarten kid who's refusing to say precisely *where* in the sandpit he buried Kylie-Jane's play lunch.

Perhaps it is Michael Small, a property developer from Runaway Bay in Queensland, who cannot live without his surfboard and whose best feature is . . . his smile. Dean Harnett, from Western Australia, has a dog called Hamish but says he's an ideal Diet Coke Guy because he's got charisma. I'm afraid that a person who describes himself as charismatic is just a little bit not. Dean does include his personality as well as his smile as best feature.

Pundee Chris Dimond, an Adelaide architecture student, says he is comfortable with himself but not arrogant. This is particularly heart rending if one happens to notice that Chris is wearing socks with sandals. (Momentarily pulls slightly ahead of field for not mentioning smile.)

Firefighter Brad Dubos from Coogee reckons his best

feature is – his smile. He thinks he's kissable. Let us not try to dissuade him as one day he may have to choose between dragging us or Eddie McGuire from a burning building.

That leaves only one possibility. Firefighter Dean Gray of Narrabeen who, when asked what he couldn't live without, says his central nervous system; when asked what makes him an ideal Diet Coke Guy, says, 'I wouldn't know how to answer this question without sounding stupid'; and, when asked for the qualities of his ideal woman, doesn't mention physical appearance at all.

Oh, just save some time and give the man a plane.

Let's just put our patooties
on the table

When I first read that the Treasurer's wife was suing Random House because it published a book by Bob Ellis that suggested she had sex, at uni, before marriage, I thought there must be more to it. Could anyone be offended by the suggestion that they used to be a bit of a goer?

Surely the concepts of chastity, virginity and 'saving yourself for marriage' are keeping company with a trilobite somewhere? Most people couldn't care less whether Tanya Costello did or didn't spend each first semester flinging herself about the quadrangle shouting, 'Hello, big boys! Come and join the Liberal Party!', wearing nothing but a platform thong. (Of course, she didn't. Get a grip.)

The point is that Mrs Costello does care. To a sincerely devout, old-fashioned Christian, what Bob Ellis wrote is insulting. And Mrs Costello has the right to be in a minority of old-fashioned, devout Christians. It's one of the things Australia's supposed to be about. It's odds on to end up in the new constitutional preamble: 'Citizens of the republic may worship their chosen religion, although that one with the goats and the chanting is pretty weird and we

do prefer Methodists' (copyright J. Howard 2007).

The decent thing for the author and the publisher to do with a Mrs Costello scenario is to apologise. And according to news reports they did not. How come people all of a sudden can't apologise, even for hurting somebody's feelings? Is it some kind of indigenous Howarditis?

Maybe they worried that an apology might be construed as an admission of liability. (When I was a cadet reporter we were forbidden to apologise to any outraged complainants. Which led to exchanges such as: 'Hello, I'm ringing about the story on page 3 with a misprint that describes me as a big fat slut with the morals of a crazed moose on Day One of the Rutting Time' – 'Thanks for sharing, sir.')

Okay, let's put our patooties on the table. I don't share Tanya Costello's morals. I've had sex with too many people.

Although, on the other hand, not enough . . . (The screen becomes swirly, we hear harp music as the protagonist takes us back to a party in 1995. 'Gosh, *he's* cute. I wonder if I should go and proposition him or go home and watch another rerun of *Columbo*? He's probably not interested, anyway.' Cut to long shot of a woman on a small couch in a small skirt, polishing off a bottle of Stoli in the winking blue light.)

I don't share Mrs Costello's religious beliefs. The Name of the Son featured very loudly in our family only when something went wrong, such as the table-tennis table collapsing on the dogs. (I was under the impression for many years that Jesus Christ had a mysterious middle name that started with H, and sometimes another less mysterious one that started with an F. Jesus first had this middle name when Flea McCrae fell off the garage roof and landed on Trevor From Two Streets Away.)

So to be perfectly upfront, I don't believe in any all-seeing, all-dancing deity – not even Gough Whitlam. (In fact, *there's* somebody who might like to, oh, call me crazy, apologise his magisterial ARSE off for being such a bubble-headed booby about East Timor, but don't hold your breath. You'll go all mauvey cobalt and then you'll kind of die.)

But what I really want to know is, will Mrs Costello's husband and all the other conservative politicians in Cabinet show the respect for a minority religious belief that has been rightly accorded to her in the courts? Or are some religious beliefs more equal than others?

When the Mirrar people of the Northern Territory

stand up before the world's courts and say, 'Our religion is all about the land, and custodianship, and passing on the stories and dreaming and customs that have evolved over thousands of years, and trying not to get nuclear waste in the ground water and stuff, and the Jabiluka uranium mine just doesn't fit into our plans', will the politicians respect it?

Or, like, not.

Ask no questions and you'll

be told no crap

Don't you simply adore little bite-size celebrity interviews? Donna Gubbay from *E! News*, asked by a tabloid what book she had read most recently, said *Hotel* by Arthur Hailey.

How much more honest than those *Vanity Fair* interviewees who say, *'Japanese Poetry* by Pamela-Zhu Bartok. It's about the sounds of grass swishing when it's alone, so alone. Brilliant.'

Possibly less honest than admitting you're so busy on the Stairmaster, eyebrow-wrangling and being photographed for *Aimless!* magazine that you haven't read anything longer than a milk carton since kinder.

The process: journalist faxes list of questions to celebrity or celebrity's publicist. Alleged style queen is asked, 'What is important to you at the moment?'

She tells glossy mag it's 'the way water shimmers on my polished-granite pond-sentinels in west Tuscany'. Instead of 'I just farted and I'm hoping nobody notices.'

'What do you love to touch?' The correct answer, it would appear, is waxed wood, raw stone, slipping the skins off baked beetroot. Under no circumstances should you

respond, 'My own private parts, actually.'

The newspaper mags are full of it.

'What are you reading/wearing/enjoying/bonking?'
'Gore Vidal/Prada beanie/the sound of rain on small brown dogs/God, he did tell me his name . . . um . . .'

'What is your favourite kitchen thing?'
'I simply couldn't go on without my industrial garlic press/Alessi lime squisher/sink hole.'

'What did you eat yesterday?'
'Breakfast, lunch and dinner/one lentil/SO much FOOD FOOD FOOD I simply couldn't recall.' (Falls away in dead faint. Carted off to closed ward.)

'Where do you shop?'
'Milan/Los Angeles/Louis Vuitton/wherever there's a cash register.'

Sour grapes? Sure, I've been *asked*. They just never print the answers.

'You're at a supermarket and you knock a stack of oranges to the floor. What do you do?'
Realising this was a cunning test of my scruples – would I walk away or clean it up? – I went one further: 'I would gather up the oranges in my calico apron and distribute them to the less fortunate.'

Didn't run it.

'What do you put in your shopping basket?'
Answered in collaboration with my radio partner, the incandescent Miss Judith Lucy, now completing her PhD in stripping at Bunny Batrouney's Bounce-'Em-'n'-Bite-'Em Barn in Vegas. 'Glitter eye shadow,' we said. 'Dental floss, in case we have to run up an emergency costume. Dried apricots because their wrinkles make us feel younger and foxier ladies.' We thought it would be more interesting than '356-grain bread because it's healthy, milk because I'm a positive person, eggs because it's good Feng Shui.'

But, no.

Never saw the light of day.

Did not print it.

The genre reached its nadir last week with elderly model Carmen Dell'Orefice, who looks like a wig on a javelin, in a Lancôme ad. Carmen, 68, was here for fashion week, darlings, and everyone thought she was simply MARVELLOUS because she was SO stylish. (Somebody that old can still be dangerously thin and wear ludicrously expensive clothes and have cosmetic surgery! How ADMIRABLE. Saturate the media at once!)

In answer to 'What did you eat yesterday?', Carmen clanged in a voice made gravelly by cigarettes or talking crap, 'I was a trained athlete and ballet dancer so I have always been aware of eating right and my diet has never really changed.' (How tremendously gratifying, especially since so many trained athletes and ballet dancers develop eating disorders so don't eat enough to menstruate and their bones become horribly brittle.)

'In my childhood I refused milk and now I have lean bones.' (No comment.)

'I had no lunch yesterday because it didn't present itself in my travels.' (Translation: 'Thank God nobody offered. I certainly wasn't going to mention it.')

'I like my fish to be served whole so I can silently give thanks to all the little fish for their nutrients.' (Of course, she's not a barking fruitcake. She is merely somewhat spiritual.)

How about some questions Carmen wasn't asked?

'When is a woman finally to be asked about her life's achievements – work, family life, interests,

attitude – not what size her faffing frock is?'

'When can she get a rest from having to be a sexy babe? Seventy, eighty?'

'And Carmen? Could you bugger off?'

Young people and the devil's shenanigans

Every time a school student goes berko with a gun in the US, the President looks shocked (which is quite a thing in itself considering his track record) and newsreaders say, 'The question that must be answered is, what can make a teenager feel so deeply?'

The question that must be answered (apart from 'Um, should we allow this troubled child to festoon his hormone-ravaged person with automatic weaponry?') is, have all these authority figures forgotten what it's like to be young? My unrequited love for Spiro Plenides rose to such a zenith that when he took Tracey Palmer to the Year 11 dance, I could have . . . anyway.

Part of being a teenager is being assailed by great, thunderingly enormous, swingeing surges of all sorts of deep emotions: hate, love, fear, self-loathing, righteous up-your-selfness, doubts about the future, humiliation, envy, unspecific morbid dread, decisions about who you are and what to do and what's worthwhile, body image . . . and then there's the confusing stuff.

All this is set against the broiling maelstrom of sudden

sexuality blaring out like a boom box in your brain, with the bass thumping further below at regular intervals. And now it's time for exams, which may determine your entire future. Plus there's anything else that may be happening, like poverty, violence, massive unemployment, a school that squashes your creativity because there's not enough teachers and services, or parents sniping at or ignoring each other, who never listen but who flick you some guilt-money if you're looking like a rabbit in the headlights.

And then you might read something like this in a recent *Australian* newspaper: 'When Barry Dickins interviewed six World War 1 veterans – all aged over 100 – he found a quiet courage sorely missing in today's youth.' Mr Dickins wrote about 'modern youth': 'Anything positive wearies them. I'm sorry, but I don't like the heroin culture of self-pity and cowardice.' Mr Dickins must be unacquainted with those crashingly tedious over-forties heroin users, daily dope heads and assorted whingeing drunks who haven't had a new thought in their heads since the seventies.

'Maybe,' Mr Dickins concludes, 'the problem with young Australians today is that they have nothing to fight for.' Unlike the poor bastards at Gallipoli who were fighting for the magnificent reason that the Poms had put them on the wrong beach and helped them only by default in failing to issue each soldier a hot-pink uniform and a plastic fork. Does anyone really doubt that if 'the young people of Australia' had to defend their country today there would be just as many cowards and just as many courageous heroes (sometimes both in the same body) as there were in the past?

Some of the blokes who came back from previous wars were scarred for life in all sorts of ways. Some, for reasons of luck to do with personal experience and psychology, 'handled it' on the surface. Others started at noises and couldn't be in crowds, or sat silently in corners of lounge rooms for years, their insides ruined by slavery camps. This lack of bravado after the fact doesn't mean they were cowards. It means they were human.

Yes, that's the bally sort of thing our young people need today to smarten them up a bit. Let those scruffy boys and girls be armed to the teeth, rev 'em up and set them at some foreigners with a bayonet in a wet, stinking trench full of despair and blood and the bits of people that nature has seen fit to shield us from with skin. Top hole.

Nearly ninety years after what we call Gallipoli, more and more young Australians and New Zealanders turn up on the other side of the world, out of the way of other tourists, at Gelibolu in Turkey where you can still see the trenches, and bullets and bones come to the surface after rain. They pay their respects in the strange silence and have a look and a think for themselves about how ghastly it must have been. And I'd rather they all had pierced tongues and blue hair and listened to shiteful music made by computers and, yes, even wore skirts over their trousers than will them into those bloody trenches.

Battle of the sexes

[less-than-exciting theme music]

HOST: Welcome back to *Battle of the Sexes*. Kimberley, how do you split an atom?

KIMBERS: Well, say you've got uranium 238 or plutonium 232 – those numbers, obviously, are the number of protons in the nucleus – you'll also need a confined, controlled space in which to bombard an unstable atom with heavy neutrons . . .

HOST: Ha ha, you girls! No, the answer is – hairspray.

KIMBERS' MATE: Awwww, bad luck, Kimbers.

HOST: Let's see what the boys can do. Wayne, where would you find the clitoris?

WAYNE: Um, Zimbabwe?

Beauty spot or fat mole?

Let's find out what's up in the beauty world, with our resident beauty expert, Princess Spakfilla von Furstenburg.

Oh. Sadly, Princess Spakfilla came in wearing pale blue eye shadow and we had to shoot her, so I'm filling in.

The new trend in cosmetics is not supermodels pouting in pretendy, long-lasting lippy, but deep thought – and groovy make-up shops like Mecca Cosmetica have imported new brands such as Philosophy.

Philosophy products have names like the Deeply Superficial Exfoliator, and the Present and Hope in a Jar, which are both moisturisers. And each one comes with some words of wisdom such as 'Choose hearts not minds, choose souls not bodies, choose grace not style, choose actions not words.' Not to mention 'Choose to get your wallet out right now and give me your credit card.'

There's another company called Stila, and they have eye shadows in cardboard boxes. When you open the boxes and look in the lids they have little mottoes like 'If it were the fashion to go naked, the face would hardly be observed' by Mary Montague. I don't know who Mary was, but she obviously knew a lot of perverts. And I bought some gold eye shadow called Irma la Douce, which says inside the lid, 'Forever is composed of nows', by poet Emily Dickinson. Which I think is far more romantic than 'Warning: eye shadow can damage your fitness and causes lung cancer.'

So, as you can see, things are getting very, very deep and meaningful in the make-up world, and it is believed that Pamela Anderson Lee is bringing out a new range of lipsticks with messages like 'Yesterday is the day before, um . . .

another day', 'Thinking is as thinking does' and 'Get another tat.'

Unsubliminal ads

[*harp music*]

WOMAN: Ladies! Tired of being a wallflower? The latest in Hoist-it's party bras will keep your bosoms going in different directions for hours. Try our pretty new East–West bra. It has new, pointy bits like ice-cream cones! Poke his eye out!

MAN: A man needs something manly to wrap around his rock-hard torso. Like a pair of Brute Trousers. Or possibly another man. That's entirely up to you. Brute Trousers. For people who want a pair of trousers. You know, to put in their closet. Brute Trousers. Big, strong, attractive, tough, yet caring – trousers. If that's what you're interested in.

Ivy's gardening tips

Hello, it's Ivy with gardening tips for February.

Now, we all know that water is a scarce commodity

during the summer months. So do your bit and restrict sprinkling the lawn to a few hours a day around midday, and only hose down the driveway on every second day.

This is the time of year when you'll be wanting to spray your fruit trees. You don't want to get any spray on your clothes, so get up there in the nuddy and give the trees a good soaking. You'll get it all over yourself and breathe it in, but I usually find the pustules go down after a few months and it's never affected my mental small, brown dog, Queenie. Not since she's been dead, certainly.

And don't neglect your lemon tree. Bludgeon any caterpillars, and wee on it constantly.

Get out.

Thoughts of motherhood

As regular readers will know, unless they have been taking crank and not paying any attention, this column is a gigantic fan of little books, those volumes of penetratingly obvious wisdoms dispensed one per page. We have written several ourselves, just for the sheer thrill of only needing 162 sentences in a book.

But we can only bow, scrape and mutter incoherently in awe at the mighty achievement of the Chronicle Book company of San Francisco, which has given us *A Box of Thoughts for Mothers*. The sheer brilliance of this publishing venture is at once obvious to the most casual observer. It is not even a book. It is a pack of tiny cards less than half the size of an average business card, with quotes on them.

When you take one quote from somebody and publish it with attribution, you are neither plagiarising nor breaching copyright laws. It is only when you steal several quotes and pretend they came out of your own dear cranium that you attract the attention of merciless, pedantic, spoilsporty fact-fetishists.

So, take a number of quotes from different people,

whack them in a tiny box and you save yourself the need
to find or pay (a) an author or (b) a bookbinder. Thus, in
A Box of Thoughts for Mothers, we have the suspiciously
named Cornelia Paddock saying, 'A mother's love perceives
no impossibilities.' Miss Paddock, it must be assumed, has
not attempted to remove watermelon stains from a white
romper suit.

Naturally, Mark Twain is quoted – it must be illegal to
release a book (or stack) of quotes without including him.
It is amazing how one can keep learning throughout life.
I had no idea that Mark Twain was a mother and thereby
eligible to comment on motherhood, but in those days
biographies shied from revealing that 'He was so busy
being pregnant or breastfeeding, the great man of literature hardly had time to menstruate during his child-
bearing years. The character of Huck Finn was fleshed out

to a stenographer during one of his caesareans.' One senses a massive cover-up.

Henry David Thoreau, another little-known mother who no doubt practised midwifery as a hobby and spent the rest of his time thinking up sternly wise things for people to scatter about in anthologies, contributes: 'We shall see but a little way if we require to understand what we see.' Poor Henry David had obviously been up all night with a toddler who had gastro when he came up with that piece of doodlery. Good on him for having a go.

'I wish you . . . some sweeter peace from the hurrying things and some closer fence from the worrying things,' adds John Ruskin, who I would be inclined to take more seriously if he hadn't, poor timorous shrieking poet, taken fright on his wedding night at the fact that his wife had pubic hair and never gone near that vicinity again. Mr Ruskin was severely traumatised by this anatomically furry departure from Rubens's paintings and illicit French water-colour postcards.

A Box of Thoughts for Mothers also canters out the obligatory 'Chinese proverb': 'It is the wise parent who gives his child roots and wings.' Although perhaps more attention to the five food groups would provide a more balanced diet.

If it was *A Box of Thoughts OF Mothers* rather than FOR them (and I include here Fathers, especially Ones at Home with the Children, but it probably wouldn't fit on the cover), it would be filled with small, scrappy bits of half-chewed Post-it notes, with barely legible scrawlings such as 'Buy milk and . . . something' and 'Sleeping. Remember sleping schelppin slipping' and 'School lunches × 5 sleepover Thursday Jason footy practice 7.30 a.m. Courtney slumber 3 parties Sunday get presents shopping kids from school kinder fete cake guttering leak dog worms get White King see what smell is in fridge change out of trackypants before wkd.' And perhaps 'Call Dreamworks re film rights.'

May you gain something from this marvellous quote from the *Box*: 'One must still have chaos in oneself to be able to give birth to a dancing star.' Friedrich Nietzsche said that. I reckon that's probably because he didn't have to imagine something pointy and hyperactive coming out of his vagina.

The answer is blowin' in the plastic bag: the Oscars telecast

Oh, dear Lordy, let there come a day lickety-split when Jack Nicholson does not sit in the front row at the Oscars ceremony, looking like a demented eye surgery patient in shades, yelling inaudible epigrams to a deferential host such as 'Yeah, hey.'

Also, Lordy of All Academy Awards Ceremonies, can you please ensure next year that someone – anyone – runs slightly amok. For what is an awards night without tears and ludicrous posturing, and people who wear flowerpots on their head. (Cher, we gave you all the best years of our lives, and this week all you can manage is a wig that could fit in a glove box.)

Give me those footy club awards nights where Robbo was legless, Vince from the take-away fell over Christine's sister-in-law and Burlo was hurlo out the back. When the best and fairest trophy gets handed out, I want some boofmeister to get up and mumble, 'Good on ya, fellas, specially coach. And, oh yeah, thanks to Mrs Vince for washin' the jumpers.'

This is brief, this is sheepish, this is incompetent and

charming. It is Australian. Note that the recipient will not thank his children, the Lordy, or 'all the people I've ever met', nor will he produce a speech on white paper the length of Botswana but still forget to thank his spouse. Many of us who viewed this week's Oscars on the telly (which went for about three weeks) were hornswoggled to see the Oscar-scooping screenwriter of *American Beauty* thanking a plastic bag he once saw blowing in the wind outside the World Trade Centre.

This is because there are some languid moments in the film portraying the ability to see beauty in the most ordinary things. A London film critic for the *Telegraph* immediately afterwards opined (I'm simply opining away for you, darlink) that the screenwriter, instead of writing a complex, thoughtful, heartfelt film (although what is

WRONG with Annette Bening's character wearing matching gardening gloves and clogs?), should simply have popped that 'useless' litter right in the rubbish bin where it belonged.

Which would make a terrific film. The movie: *Quite Hygienic Harry*. The tag line: 'In a world where tidiness is crushed, only one man can use the appropriate receptacle provided.' ('Deeply searing' – Peter Travers, *Rolling Stone*.) I mean, the possibilities are ended.

Anyway, the only discernible Oscars fashion trend was towards way-waify starlets, suspended from their hairdos, wearing dresses that had the back cut out and sewn onto the rear hem. (It was all spines, trains and haughty mobiles.) And there's a new fashion for putting your palms together and nodding, Hindu style, as if you were Mahatma Gandhi. Or Jane Fonda. Same diff.

One of the producers of *American Beauty* thanked 'all my parents', which was certainly thorough. Annette Bening looked a bit annoyed at dragging herself and some extra kilos of amniotic fluid, baby, supplementary circulatory bits and jewels all the way down to the Dorothy Chandler Pavilion (which until very recently I thought was where you see the coloured fluffy chickens at the Royal Show) to not win the best actrine Oscar. But not annoyed enough. A spot of Swank-slapping would have helped Annette. It certainly would have entertained us.

And doesn't Russell Crowe get the best dates? He went to the Golden Globe Awards with Jodie Foster, and he took the coolest-looking person on the red carpet to the Oscars – his niece. She looked terrific because she was a kid, had sunnies on and nothing to lose, and seemed like she might actually be enjoying herself. It was also unlikely that she was wearing diamonds the size of bacon burgers or would squeal, 'Oh, my god, I'm wearing a Tyler!' (Please, not a frock designed by the lead singer of Aerosmith.)

And I like to think that if Mr Crowe's niece had bumped into Jack Nicholson she would have taken one look at the Emperor's New Sunglasses and said, 'Oh grow up. You're supposed to take them off once you get inside.'

Not that I'm interested in the cults of celebrity. But, listen, I just heard that my secret idol, lifestyle guru Martha Stewart, is in Australia, so I'm off to wax a cat boat in case she calls in. I just know she'll understand my coordinated, neutrals-inspired gardening outfit. I wonder if it needs a train.

Egocentric cowbag columnist
admits all: has no point

Have you noticed how people slag off the job of columnist? Especially people who are actually (whoopsie)
columnists themselves but are at great pains to tell you
they're not THAT kind of columnist. They wouldn't tell
you about their kids or their family or force on you their
views or assessments or mention themselves AT ALL. No.
Disgrace to journalism. (Sadly, often the only thing left to
write about is how ghastly columnists are.)

And if columnists aren't slagging off the idea of being a
columnist, they're complaining how hard it is. Well, in the
words of my bosom friend, Lady Chooky Cripps, who has
a bust the size of King Island and sounds like anyone playing Lady Bracknell, 'Get stuffed the lot of you!' Here's an
honest assessment about being a columnist: it is not as nice
as being the sultan of Brunei and it's a bloody sight easier
than anything that involves digging fence holes, riveting
hub caps or processing poultry of any description.

The biggest 'problems' columnists have are (a) not
having an idea and (b) dodging the assumptions of
others. (Oh, pass me a WorkCover form.) According to

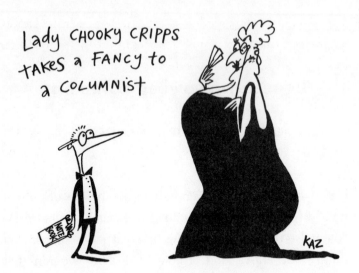

Lady CHOOKY CRIPPS TAKES a FANCY to a COLUMNIST

KAZ

correspondents, I am a feminist, woman-bashing, left-wing, Liberal-lickspittle, incendiary, ratbag, boring, vicious, namby-pamby hermaphrodite. Reminds me of that rather oxymoronic primary-school insult 'Ya frigid slut.'

It matters not how you play the game, it is how the spectators saw it, and how you played for that split second in the middle of the third quarter when a photographer was passing by. Different people catch little glimpses of you as in a cubist painting.

I'm pretty sure my dentist thinks I am a highly strung, excessively cowardly and weepy individual who makes dumb jokes in a high-pitched voice, sweats a lot and turns up on the wrong day full of Valium-related drugs.

There are people I went to parties with many years ago who would think I had slacked off a bit if all I was taking was Valium related. There are people I've been to parties with since then who think 9.15 p.m. is a tad early to be popping off home for a cocoa.

The other day I had not just a bad-hair day but a bad-me day. I was wearing a Boston Red Sox baseball cap, velvet pyjama pants, a pink corduroy shirt, a camel-coloured overcoat, knee-high socks and high-heeled brown boots tied up with ribbon. I looked a little bit like I hadn't taken my medication, which was entirely wrong as I had just come from not going to the dentist (see above) and was shopping instead. I was trying on the boots in a shoe shop, not because they were in any way attractive, but because they were ON SALE, when I fell over.

I'm not entirely sure what happened except that I had just been reminded about why I never wear high heels or take mind-altering drugs any more when the sales assistant came up and asked, 'Are you a journalist?'

'Certainly NOT madam!' I shouted. 'Just because I have taken some painkillers preparatory to a non-existent dental appointment and am badly dressed and falling down there is no need to mistake me for . . . a . . . columnist!'

'Yes, because someone up the front of the shop just recognised you,' she explained helpfully.

But of course. Because when I go out to the dentist I usually am wearing a bouffant wig and a tiara, carrying a martini and reading a copy of *Truckin' Life* magazine as you see on the back cover of this book. So completely flustered was I that I accidentally bought two pairs of Italian shoes.

Here, finally, and I think we can stop for a cut lunch, is my point: the shoe shop lady thinks I'm Imelda Marcos and the shoe shopper thinks I'm a drunken failed drag queen.

In fact, I'm a woman of many parts. I am somewhat Imelda and have also embraced my inner drunken drag queen. 'I think it's time we stopped labelling each other' is a common sentiment. I disagree. I think it would be better if we all wrote our own labels on cigarette papers, licked the sticky edge and stuck them to our foreheads so that everyone is forewarned. Mine, for example, would say 'columnist', to make used-car salesmen and real estate agents feel better about themselves.

Method acting

There's been a lot of chat about Jim Carrey's role as the short-lived comedian Andy Kaufman in the movie *Man on the Moon*. Well, except he wasn't acting just in the movie. For the duration of filming, on the set and everywhere he went, Carrey was 'in character', either as Kaufman or as a character Kaufman invented, a repellent lounge singer called Tony Clifton, who was (turn away now if you don't want to see the results) an 'asshole' (it's American for dickhead).

The thing that gets me is, everybody just accepted being treated like poop by Carrey pretending to be this Clifton guy, who yelled obscenities at people and ruined sets. Not just the people who would have lost their jobs if they didn't kowtow to this massive ego trip posing as professionalism, but even the movie's producer: 'Everybody on the set spoke to Jim as either Andy or Tony,' Danny DeVito told *US* magazine.

What I want to know is, how long do you reckon we'd get away with that sort of caper? Like *Movieline* reporter Joe Queenan, who spent a day acting like Mickey Rourke in *Barfly*, I put it to the test. For a period of some hours last

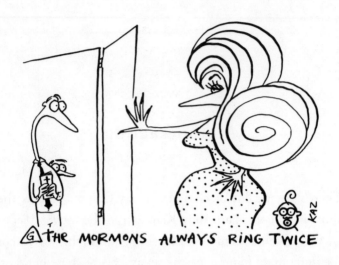

G THE MORMONS ALWAYS RING TWICE

week, I simply WAS Lauren Bacall in a gangster movie. I wore my hair over one eye, sucked long and suggestively on a fag, hoisted one eyebrow to buggery and said stuff like 'Let's drink to drinking, dangerous man. I like my drinks wet and my men dangerous' and 'You're a swell heel, and I'm cute. Care to make anything of it?' Unfortunately, the toddler wasn't interested and just kept asking for peas and a book.

'Who's this Maisy Mouse frail, anyway?' I sneered, wearing a silver shantung three-piece pants-suit with a pleated fascinator and spiked pumps. 'Some 3-year-old mouse who can't find her panda? Sure, kid. She's a bozo, but what the hell, you're a kick.' I wafted the scent of Midnight Narcissus while I took a pull on a couple of fingers of whisky, but it was no good. The Kid saw right through me. Even called me an anchor. At least, I think the Kid said anchor.

There was a knock at the door. I opened it somewhat languidly, clutching a whisky bottle in one hand, a snub-nosed pearl-handled revolver in the other.

'Hello there,' said a couple of suited-up hooch snouts in dark suits. 'We'd like to bring you today the word of our Lord.'

Suddenly I realised one of the lowlifes was Noël Coward. 'What the devil do you think you're doing, Amanda?' he barked. 'Get your tennis racquet and stop this infernal nonsense at once!'

Nuts. The jig was up.

So then I thought, there must be another character I can stay in all day, and people will indulge me and agree that, of course, I am indeed the fat little weird guy in *The Maltese Falcon*, or Daryl Hannah in *Splash*, just because I've tied my ankles together with an eel. But, hey, I'm not supposed to be an actor being someone else in a movie, I'm supposed to be an actor being someone else *for* a movie. Huh?

I s'pose there's no point pretending to be somebody's nice Aunty Dottie. Because the point of all this is you have more power if people have to put up with your being an obnoxious dunderhead. So I stuffed a side of beef down the front of my *Titanic*-worthy frock and sailed off to the milk bar.

'Silence, you ludicrous creatures!' I boomed. 'For it is I, the Countess of Bintang, Lady Chooky Cripps, scourge of the Riviera and wife to dead men in five different continents! Get me a packet of matches and 50 cents' worth of musk sticks or I'll flay you all myself!

'Furthermore, polish my jet ski! Get me the scrotum of the first assistant director nailed to a stick, and tell the producer she's an iguana in drag! I want spring water that is strained through the plaits of 9-year-old Swedish girls in matching dirndls, and PUT MY NAME ABOVE THE MOVIE TITLE or I'll bite your elbows off!'

Mr and Mrs Kim looked quite confused.

But such is the fate of the truly great artiste. I'm going to my trailer. Sure, it hasn't got a tow bar, but you've got to start somewhere.

Here's looking up your
old patio pants

May the Great Goddess of Splendour smile upon all one's dear readers who have sent one bon-bons or preposterousness that they have stumbled across. One feels so humbled (imagine one as Dame Barbara Cartland at this point, playfully hurling a small Pekinese at one's footman) that one feels compelled to share them.

Thanks are especially due to a Modern Girl we shall know only as Miss Nick – that's her first name – of Clovelly, so that strange and repellent persons (who would read this column entirely by accident) cannot look her up in the phone book and pester her with telephone queries as to the precise nature of what she may be wearing on her bottom half.

Miss Nick has sent in a truly splendid piece of nineties signage souvenired from a ladies' ablution block, to whit the following: 'Rentokil . . . To cater for your personal needs, a Sanitact Feminine Hygiene Care Service is provided. Please dispose of dressings thoughtfully.'

Dear Rentokil: dressings are for carpet burns, gunshot wounds and recreational speargun injuries. A menstrual

ACCESSORISE YOUR MARIAH CAREY PAPER DOLLY!

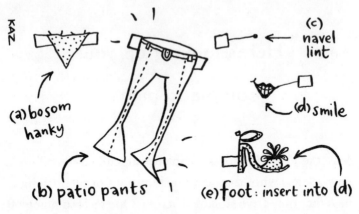

(a) bosom hanky

(b) patio pants

(c) navel lint

(d) smile

(e) foot: insert into (d)

period doesn't quite fit the bill. One is, however, frightfully grateful for the new word 'Sanitact' as it is made up of the two most important characteristics of a woman: rigidly enforced hygiene and shutuppiness.

Thank you also to the anonymous patient of a certain doctor in Frankston, who was given a typed hand-out of instructions following her hysterectomy, advising her that she was to 'refrain from indulging with your husband for six weeks'. The mind does not only boggle, it waggles, ricochets and does a couple of lazy figure eights.

Another reader, from country Victoria, poses one of the big questions of our age: 'Whatever happened 2 the Sunshine Band?' To which one must reply: nobody cares enough to find out, and perhaps you might consider seeking professional help – it is nothing to be ashamed of.

A Mr D. Boring of Vaucluse has sent one a clipping

inviting one to contribute to a right-wing magazine editor's collection of impenetrable feminist ramblings. Apparently the editor has so few examples of the genre he has appealed for assistance from the general public. Unfortunately one cannot be of any help because one only enjoys magazines with an exclamation mark in the title, such as *Hello!* and *OK!*, which are much more likely to be filled with imperturbable feminine Ramblings.

Mr Jack High (hmm) has piqued one's interest with a small newspaper report on 'England's bad boy of bowling', who 'insulted a top official'. '[Griff] Sanders was banned by his Devon county association following bad language and incidents during tournaments,' said the report. The ten-year ban was commuted to a two-year good-behaviour bond by the English (Lawn) Bowls Association.

One is indebted to the *Daily Telegraph* for the details. Griff had written 'John Smerdon is a tosser' on his score-card at the South Western County championships. Smerdon is a Devon bowls official who overlooked Griff for an important team because he used the F word. Also, he had eaten fish and chips on the green. But let us hear from Griff, who I think has encapsulated the injustice of it all: 'I thought, ten years! What have I done? I haven't done anything. I only called a bloke a tosser, right? Which in the dictionary means an obnoxious person. It's not as if I called him a wanker.'

A Mr D. Wales of New York City has sent an excerpt from the *USA Today* newspaper last month: Mariah Carey, when asked about the death of the King of Jordan, told CNN, 'I'm inconsolable at the present time. I was a very good friend of Jordan – he was probably the greatest basketball player this country has ever seen. We will never see his like again.' One of the reporters apprised Miss Carey of the until recent existence of King Hussein, and the star was gently led away 'in confusion' by her security guards, according to the paper. This was later denounced as a hoax.

Why reporters would be asking Mariah Carey about world events I don't know. She likes to be interviewed on a chaise longue wearing a bosom hanky and some spray-on patio pants. As do we all, but some of us have the washing-up to do.

Review: *In One Lifetime*

In One Lifetime is the show John Laws is hosting on the telly, which is a whole lot of historical footage strung together and a deep, sure and meaningful voice-over that has more cliches than I've had hot dinners. Or got stoned in glass houses.

And John Laws didn't even write it. He sits there and says stuff all the way through, and we get some footage at the start and the finish of him sitting there looking at us, and he looks like – I can't tell you how confronting it is to have to look at John Laws. If a woman looked like John Laws she would not be allowed within a 7-kilometre radius of a television station: they'd get out an intervention order.

Some of the footage is great – I particularly enjoyed an interview with the gorgeous Germaine Greer as a young woman in a nice frock describing how she'd been attacked by egg-throwing men when she tried to get a beer in a pub. She should have gone into comedy. But do we hear much about why women were protesting? That they got paid less for doing exactly the same jobs as blokes, that they were sacked if they got married, that they were dying from backyard abortions? No, we just get the editor of the *Women's Weekly* saying it was all a bit too strong and confronting – the sort of woman to put her own facelift in the magazine and call herself Magazine Queen.

Then Lawsie talks about how, after *Cleo* came along, we could all see Jack Thompson in the nuddy, which was a tremendous boon for women worldwide. Lawsie then recalls important Australian historical figures such as Johnny O'Keefe: 'I watched John's career . . . I was part of it.'

And, of course, a generation can remember where they were when they first heard Col Joye's first song, which Mr Laws single-handedly made a worldwide hit: 'I played it and played it . . . finally it went number one not only here but in the US and Britain as well.'

We get stock footage of protests against apartheid in the seventies and land rights marches, then the Big Trout tells us which one moral cause he felt he should stand up and support – a road tax that discriminated against truckies because truckies 'are trying in their own way to keep the dream alive'.

I don't want to be rude, but there's no need for John Laws's *In One Lifetime*. If I want to see lamb's fry in a cravat talking in cliches, I can take some hallucinogenic drugs, thanks very much.

Hoist-it ad

[*harp music*]

WOMAN: Feel like an extra few centimetres or more on
your bust line? Well, never fear, ladies, the Hoist-it
Amazement Bra is here, with 3 kilos of padding in
each cup. He need never know, if he never comes
near you! The Amazement Bra, in washable poplin!
And remember, girls, whatever your shape – if you're
a woman, it's wrong!

Ivy's gardening tips

Hello there, it's Ivy with gardening hints for March.

Rake up all the falling leaves and any old chemicals
you have around the house and set them alight in the
street. Look, they say there's a danger of explosions and
pollution, but in my day you could get dengue fever off
an American soldier soon as sleep with him so pish tosh
to that.

Identify any trees that are dropping their leaves and cut
them down with a chainsaw.

This is a good time of year to paint anything immobile
in the garden, such as concrete gnomes, the letterbox and
anyone called Stan.

Something probably needs spraying and I wouldn't hold

back if I were you. Chemicals in the garden have never done me any half a digestive biscuit and a cocoa, thanks Lorraine, I'll be in directly. Ta-ta for now.

The Bull

Episode one: the motor

Setting: the Stun Hill police station.

[The Bill *theme music*]

POLLY: 'Ere, Reg.

REG: Wotcha, Polly. Wot you got there?

POLLY: It's a villain. I arrested 'im for pinchin' a motor.

REG: Is there a subplot, Pol?

POLLY: No, Reg, not this week.

[*music out*]

Ramming it down our throat

Warning: this is not suitable reading for children until page 99.

Many diversionary methods have been employed this week to dispel the image of the Queen dressed as a giant Pine Lime Splice assuring us she feels affectionate. I tried a vintage mystery novel set in the peak pro-monarchy-era pressure-cooker world of the government-administered British button industry during World War Two.

It manages the singular achievement of revealing the murder weapon in its title: *With a Bare Bodkin* by Cyril Hare, published by Penguin in 1946. There are people in it called Mr Pettigrew and Miss Danville, and they speak 'rather archly' and finish sentences with 'I dare say.' At one point 'Edelman uttered a short, mirthless laugh.' Try that if you have a spare moment on public transport and would like some personal space.

Speaking of pressure cookers, one tried to turn from the sight of cynical reporters following the Duke of Edinburgh in case he told a disabled person to shake a leg, to embrace

the years when the Queen was always 'radiant'. I fondled the 1950 edition of *The Radiation Cookbook*, published for use with the Regulo New World Gas Cookers at a time when radiation cooking didn't conjure up images of a person in a gigantic white bee-keeping outfit holding a shrieking Geiger counter over a billy near Maralinga. Altogether now, cobbers: 'Pass the billy round boys/Don't let the pint pot stand there/For tonight they'll see the glow/From several nearby lands there.'

The subterranean message of *The Radiation Cookbook* is 'use all your parts'. It contains recipes for calf's brain fritters, roast heart ('Bake a bullock's heart for 2 hours'), stewed eel and Surprise Potatoes. (The surprise is you go to eat one and find out it's got a sausage in it.)

Speaking of using all your parts, I finally saw one of

those billboards pretending to advertise shoes but really designed to get the name of the shoe company into the paper when people point out they can't avoid seeing gigantic images of women as sexual servants. The picture on the billboard is of a man standing up and guiding the chin of a woman towards his crotch. His other hand is on his hip. The woman is sitting down with spread legs and bosoms akimbo. (To be fair, it is possible that she feels nauseous and his hand is cupped to catch any vomit.) In any case, the whole thing just screams, 'Shoes! Shoes! Shoes!'

The name of the shoes on the right side of this billboard are 'Spear', 'Snipe' and 'Stone' – all good names for characters in *The Bold and the Beautiful*. Perhaps the next range could include 'Desperate', 'Deluded' and 'Idiot'. The marketing manager of the shoe company said the woman on the billboard is 'happy doing it. She's a beautiful girl. She's such a nice person, she's confident, she's strong.' Yes, well, we all look forward to the inevitable poster next in the series, Kindly Man in Well-fitting Brogues Spontaneously Suggests Cunnilingus.

It's part of a half a million dollar advertising campaign, but it's also a mirror held up to society. I can't tell you the number of times a luminously confident, busy, half-dressed woman has remarked to me on public transport, 'I was going home to have a Lean Cuisine, a Tim Tam and a bath, but I think I'll just get off at the next stop, get on my knees and beg the first man who comes along to let me shove my face in his crotch. Nothing I enjoy more.' She's so strong.

This week I received an insulting, impertinent and male-pleasure-only-obsessed letter from a journalist at a women's magazine called *B*. She asked for a contribution to an article called '50 of the Hottest Sex Tips': 'What we're after is your own sex secret that guarantees to drive a man wild. We could either run a straight quote or, if it's something more complicated, we can run a short, step-by-step guide. Preferably we're after something physical that a woman can do to a man (eg a "Fire and Ice" blow job – the signature move of a certain high-class escort agency!).' My giddy aunt.

Here's a tip for dealing with the lot of them: utter a short, mirthless laugh.

In space no one can hear you crash

I was just a wee Barbie-doll fancier when men stomped about on the moon for the first time, but I think the message was pretty clear. Not only was it 'one step for man' and another one for 'mankind', the whole shebang looked a bit like the keg area at a barbecue and you didn't have to be a rocket scientist (oh, hardy har) to work out that there wasn't much equal opportunity employment policy going on at NASA.

Which is why you have to admire all those girlie engineers and astronauts we've been seeing in televised press conferences and, well, rocket scientists for argy-bargying their way into the driver's seat of the dune buggy of life. It's very fine to see someone on telly with a Patty Duke hairdo explaining to a bunch of slack-jawed reporters how jet propulsion works, using a scale model of something shiny. But excuse me if I nod off about the time they first say 'pod'.

Who cannot confess to a certain unseemly cynicism every time another space mission is a complete fiasco? What a shame that many of those girlie spokes-boffins

recently were forced to gesture sadly at their scale-model podettes at NASA's Jet Propulsion and Space Littering Facility and say things like 'Well, the mission isn't a total failure. It's just that a $165-million pod has buggered off into oblivion' and 'The Mars polar lander has probably crashed. Or it's sulking. It's certainly not answering the phone.'

This was not a good look after the Mars climate orbiter thingie, a shemozzly disaster, which brings the amount of money spent on these two projects to $558 million. The climate orbiter, looking a little like a cheese grater with a couple of solar panels, whizzed off to see if it was raining on Mars and then, uh, exploded into a trazillion pieces. This had something to do with some engineers measuring bits of it in metric and some who had measured bits of it in imperial increments.

Let us not dwell upon the space shuttle program.

There was that Hubble telescope that took worse pictures than a conga line of drunks repeatedly stepping on a throwaway camera during a stacks-on under a mirror ball. Even when they can get it to go right, it can be so boring you'd rather rub emery boards on your eyeballs than take any notice of it. When they do get some podlet to go up there and twang the right antenna, the pictures are still of what looks like the contents of a vacuum-cleaner bag chucked over a post-nuclear wasteland.

The colour photos of those joints in space might as well be in black and white, except the ones of Mars, which are actually taken out the back of Broome. NASA gang, you've got to face it: up close, most of the solar system looks like a poxy desert caravan site without a rec room. And Jupiter doesn't even have rocks because it's just gas. Get some therapy and stop sending defective bits of expensive aluminium joinery to a place we don't need to know anything more about. Mars is a bloody long way away and when you get there you can't have an ice cream. End o' story.

Thank heavens NASA stuff-ups have provided so much work for spin doctors. Now they're all scurrying around explaining why the polar lander may not have landed; although they're certainly not suggesting it be called the Polar Crasher or the Great Big Polar Bingle Project or Whack a Planet. No, they're saying the thing should have had $200-million airbags. They're saying it should have at least had a communications system on board so it could

ring up the control room and say, 'Youse have all completely buggered it', just before smashing into a reddish
dusty rock (surprise!). This, say experts, would have at least
let them know what to fix for the next one. The NEXT
one?!

Yes, if at first you don't succeed, chuck in another few
hundred million. As the polar lander's vice-president of
engineering said, 'We have no interest in backing off. It's
too much fun.' For heaven's sake, man, have a couple of
beers and take in a movie. You'll get change from a twenty.

Two things are bothering us

One: triangular headkerchiefs

Many young ladies are wearing those little bandannas on their heads with the triangular pointy bit flapping away on top. It is a tiny step up from tying each hanky corner in a knot. It only just beats erecting a small flagpole in your hairdo and running up a hanky to see if anyone will salute.

Obviously it's not as strong a medical health issue as Killer Platform Shoes. I'm as worried about Naomi Campbell's ankles as the next person, but this headkerchief business is a concern. People who've run out of things to do with their eyebrows and have turned in desperation to the hanky-head look must face facts: the only things that can further accessorise a headscarf are a bucket of Jif, being married to Noah or a tragic home-perming incident.

You look like a bunch of demented fundamentalist Christians in crop tops. The only place a clean hanky belongs is tucked under your bra strap. Don't you ever listen to your nanna?

BaD FASHION LOOKS

① HaNKY oN Head   ② UNDiES oN HEad   ③ fAUNA oN HEAd

Two: married men who pretend they're slightly not

Let's examine the hypothetical case of a person known to this column who has recently had the inside of her brain given a good scouring by one who wore the cloak of Recently Separated and Madly in Love with Her, only to be unmasked (shut up about the metaphors) and revealed in smouldering jocks, as in 'Liar, Liar, Your Pants Are a Four-Alarm Fire'.

For Mr Vile Swamp-dwelling Scum-sucking Beast toyed with the affections of a smart and gorgeous woman whose very soul is tinged with the love of all creatures, et cetera, et cetera, et cetera. It was only during the recent school holidays (*quelle coïncidence, mon petit merdehead*) that it became clear, through a series of investigations by agents of Miss Gorgeous (for that is what we shall call her), that Mr Toad-featured Poophead (for that is one of the things we shall be calling him) had not, as stated during the pre-liminaries, really left his wife at all.

Perhaps when he said he had left his wife it wasn't really a lie. Perhaps he just accidentally left off the end of the sentence, such as 'Some time ago I left my wife . . . to pop down the milk bar for a packet of murdered baby seal paws.' (For why should his cruelty to humans restrict him elsewhere?) Perhaps he really meant to say, 'I have left my wife . . . with the children for a sec, so I can continue my habit of romancing other women, declaring my love for them, and then dashing their hearts into teeny tiny pieces.'

It would have been accepted with sadness and some shock had he informed Miss Gorgeous of the adjusted circumstances. But he simply stepped outside one day and never returned calls.

Perhaps his confusion at this difficult emotional time caused him to become so addled that, whenever he saw a telephone, he thought it was some sort of ornamental ginger plant. This would account for Mr Weaseldick Filth-bucket being unable to pick one up and facilitate a situation in which Miss Gorgeous was finally put in the picture: he had been telling her she was the cat's pyjamas but he would prefer to treat her as kitty litter.

Far better, thought Captain Arsehole d'Taunting, to let a woman twist in the wind, worrying first that he had been gored to death by a clumsy wart-hog, then slowly realising that he was, instead, a liar and a coward, and beginning to search for the number of Dial a Goring Wart-hog.

Mr Bastardy Fraudopants has dishonoured his family and the male sex. He is a fool and a charlatan whose lack of character will forever be a stain upon his person, and he's lucky we haven't put a picture of him right here to warn others.

In closing may I just leave you with an authorisation: if you meet a morally bereft married man, you may set about his head with a sockful of sand. Remove headkerchief as necessary.

Casino!

Episode two
of our searing radio drama

[fade up thrilling theme music]
ANNOUNCER: Coming up soon on *Foxy Ladies*, it's the
unrivalled drama of our exclusive radio serial,
Casino! Yes, it's *Casino!* Starring:

>   **Phyllida Merkin** as Lady Chooky Cripps
>   **Buffy Barrymore** as Lizzie Goody Good
>   **Jane Staunch** as Joan Hack
>   **Damon Whanger** as John Goody Good
>   **and introducing –**
>   **Binky Machismo** as Dash Trowel.

Stay tuned for *Casino!*
[theme music ends]

ANNOUNCER: Last week on *Casino!* you heard John
Goody Good say –

JOHN GOODY GOOD: Look out! She's got an iceberg and she's not afraid to use it! Oh, hello, Bunty.

ANNOUNCER: And now we rejoin the splendid cast of *Casino!* as failed actress Joan Hack corners Dash Trowel, private dick, in the Fleecing Room.

JOAN HACK: I need a change from my tragic one-woman show entitled *I Don't Suppose Anyone in the Audience Fancies a Root?* Do you need an assistant in the detecting biz, Dash? Hi, Bunty.

DASH TROWEL: I don't think so, Joan. Not unless you're the sort of frail who knows how Lizzie Goody Good lost her legs. Evening, Bunty.

JOAN: Oh, it was some sort of an accident in Africa with her husband, John Goody Good, the explorer.

DASH: Is that what he told the poor dame? Look out!

LIZZIE GOODY GOOD: Look, I found John! Where have you been for two days, John? Oh, never mind, darling! Hello, Bunty. John! What a lovely axe you're carrying! Is it for me?

JOHN: You might say that. Oh, hello, Bunty. How about a turn around the balcony, Lizzie?

LIZZIE: Darling, what a spifflicatingly good idea. It's just that I . . . I don't seem to have any legs.

JOHN: No matter. Come on, old girl. As I've said
             before, chop chop!

DASH: Care for a spin on the balcony yourself, Joan?

JOAN: Mindless sex is my line, but I suppose I could
             make an exception in your case.

LADY CHOOKY CRIPPS: He's wasted on you, you
             amateur jezebel. I could have him on toast
             and still need kippers!

DASH: Ladies, please.

JOAN: Who are you calling a lady, shamus? It takes
             one to know one.

DASH: I told you never to speak of that!

ANNOUNCER: Tune in to *Casino!* next week, when
             you'll hear Joan Hack say –

JOAN: Look out, Dash! John Goody Good has a gun
             in his pocket!

LADY CHOOKY: No, I think you'll find he's just
             pleased to see me. And who the flaming pork
             haunches is Bunty?!

[*music out*]

A hang-up

Is there a more insincere sentence in the English language than 'Your call is important to us. It has been placed in a queue, and the first available operator . . .'? (I don't know what comes after that, because I'm usually SHOUTING.)

Why not just be honest: 'The first available operator is Kylie on Rottnest Island because we've laid off everyone else and she's got 500 calls on hold and, anyway, she hasn't finished her geography homework and her mum wants her to set the table and she's also responsible for customs, excise and the Defence budget', or to put it another way 'Juuust bugger OFF!'

And what is *this* about: 'When you have recorded your message, press hash or just hang up'? Lordy, there's a concept: when you've finished with the phone, hang it up. (I usually just pop the handset down my undies and kind of undulate.)

This is why the much-anticipated Email Virus Pandemic Thingie (technical term) is a grouse idea and can't come soon enough.

If all the computers fall over, maybe we could employ some real . . . damn. What are they called again? People.

People who won't say, 'Press one if there's an emergency that might be costing US money. Press two if you want to send us some more of your money for a service we are not currently providing you. Press three if you'd like to register for dealing with us only by pressing numbers on your phone so we NEVER have to deal with you again.'

Then come four hours of instrumental bon-bons presented by a member of the Iglesias family. After which, during 'The Power of Love' extended remix, you can put the phone down, make a cup of tea, familiarise yourself with the history of the Balkans situation, grow some tomatoes, make a Waldorf salad and fashion a scale model of an FA-18 from a buff envelope.

Some time later, if fully conscious, you'll get another round of options: 'Press one if you're fed up to pussy's bow but you can't hang up. Press two if you'd like a copy of our tremendously diverting publication bound in attractive polypropylene, *The Customer is Always Right in the Bloody Way.*'

At this point the computer voice will tell you the company's fax number for a machine that feeds messages straight out into the bottom of the CEO's canary cage. The recorded message will never divulge the secret location of the office concerned; for argument's sake, Telstra, Medicare, Centrelink, private health insurers, banks, power companies of any description, government departments of anything and ginormous corporations.

Perhaps there are no headquarters any more. Just four small Portaloos in Broken Hill, each staffed by someone who still plays under-13 netball and answers the phones of every entity in the entire country. (The rest of the workforce is doing permanent part-time work with no holiday pay, no sick pay, no maternity leave and split shifts akimbo, and is called Marlene.)

And when the heavens part and the angels go completely sick, and you get through to a real person . . . they can't help you. Because the computer says your problem doesn't exist. Because the computer has sent it to the wrong address. Because the computer can only handle problems with eight or fewer variants (and since when have you had one of THOSE?).

Because you cannot appeal to a computer's reason. Or make it laugh, or understand that because it put an apostrophe in the wrong place you haven't got any lunch money or that the 4-year-old threw up guacamole on the form, or get it to put you through to a supervisor. Because the supervisor is – wah-hey! – a computer.

Heaps of big-company PR people are going to call me and insist that their whizz-bang customer service system (customer what?) has increased 'productivity'. They'll send wobbly stats about the average waiting time on hold. They'll ring up and say it's stupid to wish a computer disaster on us, and that all the above is simplistic drivel written by a Luddite.

And you know, guys: your call is important to us. We just couldn't be stuffed actually answering it.

Dear possibly gay young person

(especially in the bush)

You may have heard that some archbishop or other thinks that being romantically or sexually attracted to people of the same sex is dangerous and terrible and can lead to suicide. This is what some archbishops think they are for. They thunder around the place during the week telling people to stop it or they'll go blind, and then get all gussied up in a pointy hat and a frock for Sunday and do it all again standing on a box. It is really very boring of them.

The truth is, what can lead to suicide is feeling alone and trapped and persecuted and despairing. Like when you think you might be gay, and if they suspected everyone would hate you and make your life hell. You might think, 'What if I don't grow out of it and can people tell by looking and I can't seem to make myself change and I must be an evil person.' Yes, well, that's what you get for listening to ning-nong archbishops.

Thankfully there is help at hand! Hurrah! Is it the bold and well-accessorised Pooftaman, in lime-green sling-backs, clutching a picture of Tinky Winky Teletubbie, who will come to your parents and have at them with a handbag

GAY SHEEP-CRUTCHERS' NETWORK

until they get it? Is it bravely gorgeous old henna-head Lezzogirl, who shall appear in a puff of purple lipstick and Cuban-heeled dancing shoes and take you away in a designer pumpkin? Thankfully nothing so ostentatious. (Unless you ask nicely.)

Because, even though you might live in a place where nobody ever talks about homosexuality except to make nervous little jokes about it ('Ha ha ha ha, good one, Robbo' – punch Robbo in head to indicate heartfelt yet manly affection), elsewhere there are seething masses of gay people just waiting for your call. Okay, they're not actually literally waiting for your call because they have lives to get on with, like being judges and doctors and mechanics and farmers and shop assistants; computer folk and teachers and hairdressers (no, really); and labourers and politicians and footy players and mums and dads.

Some of them are hilarious screaming nancy boys who get dressed up in frocks and pretend they're Shirley Bassey. And some are grown women who like to wear strappy leather cowgirlie things, with fringes on them, and show their bosoms at nightclubs. But if that doesn't float your boat you could be a quiet telephonist. Or both. Or even one of those gay persons who are 'out' with their friends but who don't tell workmates or parents for a long time (or ever). (Although there's a group for parents of gay people who don't mind and it's got lots of members, and there are plenty of workplaces where it doesn't matter if you've got a girlfriend or a boyfriend or a pet blue-tongue called Barry-Anne.)

Gay people mostly have the same problems as straight people, like broken hearts and having to have safe sex so they don't get a sexually transmitted disease. Oh, it gets worse – they have to pay the rent and find a pair of matching socks in the morning.

Of course, you may not be gay at all. You may just be thinking about it for a while, maybe even do a bit of experimenting before going straight. But if you are gay it's not something you choose. It's just something you are. And that something is not hateful or necessarily dangerous. What's dangerous is being told that it's hateful, or that you can make it go away with willpower or psychiatry or by punching Robbo.

Much better to find somewhere where it's fun. We're out here – the gay, the friends of gay, the couldn't give a stuff if you're gay. When you're ready, come and say hello. But don't despair and don't feel alone. All over the world and within a train ride of your place there are gay book-shops, gay video shops, gay nightclubs, Mardi Gras marchers, gay churches, elderly gay hairy fat people groups, gay young heavy-metal fanciers, the plain and dull gay folk network: there's bound to be a gay sheep-crutcher's support group if you look hard enough.

As a matter of fact we outnumber feral archbishops by millions to one.

Gay and lesbian counselling lines: there's one in your area. Look in the White Pages, or call Lifeline and get the number from them.

Crankypants: the justice department

Why am I feeling a bit crankypants? I've been worrying about Lady Sonia McMahon. As you know, I feel very deeply for these ladies with berzillions of dollars who run into trouble with the law, and Lady Sonia was back in court this week. You'll recall how distraught I was when poor Lady Susan Renouf finally noticed that her housekeeper had lifted about half a million bucks' worth of jewels. Lady Susan was finally alerted – after about a year – to the cunning thievery when she noticed one of her necklaces around the neck of another very rich lady at a society do. And clearly had the breeding not to wrestle the woman to the ground shrieking, 'Give me back my sparklies, you slack moll.' That's class.

And now look what's happened to her colleague, Lady Sonia McMahon, with a face tighter than a wing nut on an aircraft carrier. It takes an effort to be blonde when you're in your seventies. Lady Sonia McMahon has had a shocking week. I mean all she was doing was driving a car when she was completely and utterly rat-faced drunk.

Now, where's the harm in that, if you're a rich woman in

a very nice car who will turn up to charity dos and get her picture in the magazines? I mean, fair's fair, Lady Sonia is a pillar of the community, which as you know means she stands around looking a bit architectural. I mean, double the blood alcohol limit? Big deal. Thankfully the magistrate realised quality all the way and let her off. I mean, you can't fine rich people – they wouldn't notice. And you can't put them in jail – what would they wear? And you can't cancel their driving licence because then how would they get to the bank?

Hoist-it ad

[*harp music*]

WOMAN: Ladies, our new strapless Hoist-it bra incorporates side panelling! Twist-away sprauncers! And oomph-elastic under-phoofers on each bosom! Yes, there'll be no slipping in your pretty new Gravity Buster – with extra gaffer tape free. Detachable whim-whammer on request.

Ivy's gardening tips

Hello, it's Ivy with gardening tips for April.

You should have your bulbs and your false teeth in by

now, it's gone 9 o'clock. Make sure your daffs are in the right way up or they'll explode in the night like home-brew.

Right. Hydrangeas. Don't bother. You can get perfectly good plastic ones at Kmart. Same goes for trees in general. Plant some car tyres halfway into the dirt and paint them white – makes a lovely border.

Finally, don't be shy with herbicides. The ones used in the Indochinese wars are the best, I find. I've been using them for years and I'm perfectly five bucks on Hullabaloo Lad in the fourth at Warwick Farm, thanks darl.

Cheerio.

The Bull

Episode two: women

[The Bill *theme music*]

NORIKA: 'Ere, Tosh.

TOSH: Yes, Norika.

NORIKA: I'm a WPC, Tosh.

TOSH: Wot's that then, Norika?

NORIKA: Woman Police Constable, Tosh.

TOSH: Luckily the police force is not in any way sexist, then.

NORIKA: That's right.

TOSH: Cuppa tea thanks, pet.

[*music out*]

Throw another jacket on the Barbie

Perusers of supermarket checkout displays will be familiar with the standard array of Kit Kats, *Who Weekly*'s 100 Most Infuriating People Who Are Already Famous, and Little Golden Books. One of their biggest-ever sellers is *The Poky Little Puppy*. I am unqualified to comment on the puppy's pokiness, but I'm pretty sold on another Little Golden Book I found.

On the back it says: 'We salute the talented authors and artists who create the books.' I couldn't agree more after reading *Barbie: In the Spotlight*, a Little Golden Book that is made up of text and photographs of a Barbie doll and a few other very similar dolls, some of which have pretendy goatees and look to have recently failed a Village People audition.

Barbie is the star, and she is wearing a black miniskirt, black high-heeled pumps and a faux Chanel jacket. If you're not familiar with the faux Chanel jacket, think Nancy Reagan or any of those emaciated, repulsively wealthy women who look like baby birds with papier-mâché piñata heads. The bumpy texture of the fabric is not

dissimilar to that of on-site caravan upholstery and I think is called bouclé.

Anyway, Barbie is, of course, a television reporter, and she goes to interview a new fashion designer called Kelvin (my guess is his mates Craig And Huddo For Yves St Laurent will be chartreuse with envy). GUESS WHAT? Barbie has to step in and be the model instead of finishing her story, so her sister Skipper becomes the reporter (which is how most of us started).

Thankfully Skipper turns out to be a sister who has brought two friends, because in the previous pages it seemed that Barbie was being stalked by a badly dressed cult. Skipper wears a coordinated outfit of lime-green twin-set, miniskirt and high-heeled shoes with gigantic flat daisies on them. Also, her long, blonde hair goes all the way down to her bum, and she looks like someone has just this moment sucked all her brains out of her left ear with a reverse-thrust leaf blower.

One of the problems with using still photos of posed dolls is that the dolls have no expression on their face whatsoever. (At least the *Thunderbirds* people have feral eyebrows.) The same lobotomised look can accompany lines such as 'How would you advise the United Nations to respond to the Congo situation?', 'Look out! It's a woman in flat shoes!' and 'Barbie, your arse is on fire and Ken's got your head in a bowling bag.'

(Lawyer's note: None of these lines appear in any Little Golden Books.)

Every character looks like it has been dressed and designed by a screaming nancy boy who hasn't taken his lithium. This is disturbing because there is no list of credits and I would very much like to get in touch with that screaming nancy boy and be his new best friend. It has certainly whetted my appetite for some of the other titles in the Little Golden Book range such as *Very Busy Barbie*, *Trail Blazer Barbie* and *Barbie: The Big Splash*, although not as much as I'd like to see *Rather Slovenly Barbie*, *Unambitious Barbie* and *Barbie: The Surprisingly Slack Moll*.

(Lawyer's note: OH, MY GOD. See previous advisement.)

I shall certainly be keeping an eye out for the *Little Golden Book About God*, which I hope will be illustrated with pictures of small magnetised dashboard saints arranged around a balsawood card table for the Last Supper. I am also not very happy about the idea of *Winnie the Pooh: Eeyore, Be Happy!* as it could create a precedent and spawn other ironic literary spin-offs such as *Lady Macbeth, Get a Grip!*; *The Muddle-headed Wombat: Read Edward De Bono!*; and even *Alice Doesn't Go Anywhere Near a Looking Glass and Gets Her Homework Done!*.

Little Golden Books blurb writers suggest the books promote literacy. I simply put to you, is it worth it? Do the ends justify the means? And when Barbie says, 'Reporting on International Fashion Week is so exciting. An assignment like this makes my job interesting', why doesn't someone hold her down and snap her arms off?

Okay, Your Holiness,

so what's the punchline?

Hey, guess what? I've just received a personal email from the Dalai Lama. I know what you're thinking – Lordy, I s'pose Nelson Mandela sends her postcards all the time, Xanana Gusmao pesters her with knock-knock jokes by fax and Madeleine Albright won't get off the walkie-talkie. Yep.

But the email from this Dalai Lama (as opposed to the Dalai Laa Laa, who is a Teletubbie in a saffron robe) did not have his usual insouciant charm, and certainly lacked the customary 'How's it hangin'?' style greeting from this dispossessed yet perky world leader.

'Happy 2000 from the Dalai Lama. The following is taken from a Nepalese Good Luck Mantra. You'll find it to be worth reading and worth sharing. [Note unusually imperious tone.] Do not keep this message. The mantra must leave your hands within 96 hours. [Presumably His Holiness learned to talk this way when he was an extra in *Mission Impossible* 2.] You will get a very pleasant surprise.' Universal justice, maybe? A boutique sales assistant who says, 'Don't buy that, it makes your arse look like the Bungle Bungles'? An Aboriginal Affairs minister with more sense than a Besser brick?

THE DALAI LAA LAA

uh-oh, China

Kaz

Working on Grandma's motto, which was 'Ain't you never took a risk, lady?' (as opposed to Nanna's favourite, a dead heat between 'Keep Yourself Nice' and 'There's nothing very clever about being clever'), I am passing on these Dalai Lama-ish platitudes.

'When you lose, don't lose the lesson.'
(And the lesson is: you lose.)

'Follow the three Rs: respect for self, respect for others and responsibility for all your actions.'
(Or alternatively you may follow the three Bs: bottle up and go, baby please attend to my flammable needs, and bugger the consequences.)

'Remember that not getting what you want is sometimes a wonderful stroke of luck.'

(This often applies to people with holiday homes at Sorrento who thought they were being given a Li-Lo for Christmas and got an amphibious Mercedes, and is a less-frequently recognised phenomenon in Mali, Australian immigration detention centres and Tennant Creek.)

'Learn the rules so you know how to break them properly.'

(An accountant and a lawyer with the morals of a plankton will help.)

'Don't let a little dispute injure a great friendship.'

(Unless, of course, you are an oil-producing nation that sells to North America.)

'When you realise you've made a mistake, take immediate steps to correct it.'

(Or you could simply scream in a very high-pitched voice and then cover your eyes.)

'Spend some time alone every day.'

(If you are a parent working at home with small children, you may emit an ironic barking sound now.)

'Open your arms to change, but don't let go of your values.'
(And, please, try some antiperspirant.)

'Remember that silence is sometimes the best answer.'
(Especially if you're a dunderhead.)

'Live a good, honourable life. Then when you get older and think back, you'll be able to enjoy it a second time.'
(Oh, THAT'S why I'm living on a cut-price pension, with some second-hand trousers that do up under my armpits.)

(Some other mantra sentences go here but I nodded off.)

'Once a year, go some place you've never been before.'
(Yeah, like Liechtenstein or into a Torana boot.)

(Some more napping here.)

'Approach love and cooking with reckless abandon.'
(Why not seek out relationships with people who are addicted to chrome sniffing, and flambé some fugu blowfish over a gas flame hooked up by Snookums, who is consulting a 1927 plumbing handbook while free-basing.)

At the end it says if you email this list to fewer than five people your life will improve slightly; to five to nine people your
life will improve to your liking; to nine to fourteen you will
have at least five surprises in the next three weeks; to fifteen
or more people your life will improve 'drastically and everything you ever dreamed of will begin to take shape . . .
regards, Dalai Lama.'

Review: *Gloss* magazine

Let's take a wee look at the launch issue of *Gloss* anti-ageing magazine.

Chase Asten, make-up artiste, 'has created beautiful faces for Jerry Hall, Cameron Diaz and Kate Winslet.'

Because, of course, their own faces look like baboon arses.

I imagine he uses papier-mâché and a bit of spit.

'Chase is a make-up genius and his mantra of the moment is "pretty, pretty, pretty".' (It used to be 'hideous, hideous, hideous', but his career stalled.)

Here's another sample of *Gloss* copy: 'You love your mum. Sure you do. But be honest. Have you ever noticed the Serious Crow's Feet problem she has? Winced at the way her chin triples itself? Ever thought quietly to yourself heck, I hope I don't take after her . . .'

When I look at my mum, I don't think good on her for looking after the bubba this afternoon, and maybe she'd like a cup of tea and a discussion avoiding most of the pitfalls of the mother–daughter relationship minefield. No, I always think, 'Why don't you look a bit more like Claudia Schiffer?'

Gloss has articles on permanent make-up (anything that makes you look a little bit more like Michael Jackson has got to be a good thing); and oxygen puffed onto your skin – 'Lack of oxygen has been linked with disease.' Well ectually, darlink, lack of oxygen has been associated with 100 per cent of dead people, but that's no reason to blast it onto your face in the hope that it will make you ten years younger – especially if you look 10 years old like the models in this magazine.

An article suggests that one 'revel in the luxury of being home alone with a baby': this is a fashion spread in which a pouting young woman spends the time her baby is asleep (which must be, like, HOURS), wafting round in various zebra-print outfits and floating gerberas on the surface of her in-ground swimming pool to amuse the baby when it wakes up. Which pretty much describes my day.

Personality tests

Whenever I read in the paper that somebody has been remanded in custody pending psychiatric assessment, I always wonder why they need to go to all that expense.

Why not just get the person to do the *Cosmo* quiz? Are you too fat? Are you good girlfriend material? Are you SURE you're not too fat? And do you have homicidal tendencies?

Or why not just check the horoscope scrolls from the chemist? 27 October: you will probably try to do over a TAB, dressed in a nylon pants-suit, and get done like a dinner by a passing probationary constable.

Ivy's gardening tips

Hello, and welcome to Ivy's gardening hints for May.

A friend of mine, Bon Scott, used to come over here of an evening, take a bit of speed, have a few slabs and some Jim Beam and say to me, 'Ivy, the begonias are looking fuckin' great, but what you need is a bit of snail bait.' And I kept forgetting. So Bon made up a little rhyme to remind me when to get snail bait at the hypermarket. It goes something like this:

> [*to tune of AC/DC's 'Jailbreak'*]
> Snails! [*guitar*] They were racin'!
> Freedom! [*sound effects*] They was chasin'!
> Porchlights! [*sound effects*] Sirens! [*sound effects*] Pellets!
>   [*sound effects*] Firin'! [*sound effects*]
> The snails shrivelled up . . . leaving just the shell off
>   their BACK!
> SNAIIIL BAIT! SNAIIIL BAIT!
> SNAIIIL BAIT!
> [*guitar, et cetera out*]

Hoist-it ad

[*harp music*]

WOMAN: Girls, it's a new century, and you know what that means! Back to the fifties with fashion. Get yourself a brand-new Hoist-it Waspie that will give you a teeny waist in seconds! Prehensile steel with midriff-remover panels! It will shove that spare tyre around your waist right up under your bosoms! If your ovaries are insured, you can't go past a Waspie!

The Bull

Episode three: surrealist poet

[The Bill *theme music*]

POLLY: Sierra Oscar, Sierra Oscar to Sergeant Cryer.

SERGEANT CRYER: Hello, Polly. Who's Sierra Oscar?

POLLY: I dunno, Guv. I fink he was a Portuguese surrealist poet in the twenties.

SGT CRYER: You wot?

[*music out*]

Farmophobia

Some farmers are complaining about the way they have been treated in an ad that shows a farmer doing stupid things and saying 'Bugger!' Well, get in line, ya gumboot-wearin' stem-o'-wheat-chewin' laconic flannelette-shirt-wearin' salt-of-the-earth weather-beaten crows'-feet-sportin' horizon-scannin' hat-brandishin' stereotypes.

Where were yez when they had that ad of the dairy farmer in aforementioned gumboots runnin' thousands of moiles to the city with a spoonful o' milk to put in the mega-fat milk carton, eh? How stupid was that? Did we hear a peep out of yez then? Nope. (I'm talkin' like farmers are s'posed to, y'know, in th'ads on the flippin' telly.)

And what about the fact that farmers are always portrayed as slightly twinkly blokes over 50, with grey hair and regulation gumboots? Where are the women farmers, the younger farmers? I'm not suggesting that Kellogg's bring in a lesbian Zimbabwean chook-sexer for their next ad but, jeez, why the late start with the complaints that those Toyota HiLux 'Bugger!' ads don't represent the full diversity of intellectually able farming folk?

For all I know most farmers are deep thinkers who write poems rhyming 'masculinity' with 'salinity'. But where was the poultry industry when that Toyota chicken kept crossing the bloody road instead of being restrained with decent fencing by its rightful owner? What about those years of ads with farmers who care more about beer than anything else and stand round on verandahs waiting to be visibly aroused by words like 'bewdy', 'g'day' and 'one tonne'?

I mean, how do you think women feel after years of being portrayed as shiny-haired, neck-swivelling poppets with all the brains of a mollusc with a head injury (I don't care if molluscs don't have heads. Who do you think you are – David Attenborough? I'm trying to get up a metaphorical thingie here), or margarine-addicted martyrs with wry smiles who can be relied upon when given a box of Cadbury Roses chocolates to display such intense gratitude that their heads simply fly off their necks and into the ironing basket?

Furthermore, how about that Australia Post ad where the actor goes in to pay a bill and (get out the hospital brandy) THERE IS NO QUEUE? Not to mention it's an actual post office, not the usual newsagency–knick-knacks post office the size of a B4 envelope with queues estimated at the length of the equator.

Where is the farming fury over the Emporio Armani ads for his and her perfumes called something like 'Him' and 'She' in three different languages? The one where it's all in black and white and extraordinarily well-groomed young adults are clutching each other and saying things like 'She's perfect' and 'She's mine' and 'He likes to be touched' in dreamy voices, and nobody comes into shot and tells them to take a good hard look at themselves? Is this not an affront to reality?

Is it any worse than the ad for aftershave in which some moody, chiselled-chin-sporter looks like he's having a sort of sulk where he refuses to say much more than 'Hugo. Dark Blue'? Why is he not on medication? What about the guy who gets released from a chain gang and then comes back and eats a hamburger in front of his former colleagues? Surely this was supposed to screen in Louisiana and there was some sort of fiasco with the padded bags?

What about the ad where a kid isn't doing well at school

so, instead of talking to him about it, the parents buy him computer hardware to let him churn out school projects like coffee-table books? Just a high-tech version of the seventy-two pack of Derwent coloured pencils if you ask me. A multicoloured margin didn't save a crap idea in the olden days, and a colour printer does not a thinker make.

The only true-to-life ad on telly is the one where a leopard and a crocodile are on some sort of pontoon having a chat and then the croc eats a passing jet skier. Laughs, social justice, and there's not a farmer in sight. But buggered if I can remember what it's for.

Nudey Plump Chicks with a Caesarean Scar Monthly magazine

Once again, we position the driftnet over the mailbag, shake the bag out on deck and see what divine little squidlets have come up from the postal briny with the heaving, leviathan, mammalian . . . You know, I sometimes find that a metaphor gets entirely out of control and it's best for everyone to just abandon the sentence while you still have time, before the peeved, swirling, gelatinous seas rise in ludicrous waves of . . .

So, anyway, our correspondent Kathrin of Wahroonga (which sounds rather more like a rude car-horn noise than a suburb) dragged herself kicking and screaming recently from a Queen Victoria Building fashion parade in Sydney to inquire, 'In this conformist fashion mode, if the model isn't wearing a hat or a fur, how does one tell whether she is wearing a nightie or an evening dress?' We here at *Aussie Style Big-format Black and White Nudey Plump Chicks with a Caesarean Scar Monthly* magazine are happy to oblige. Our advertising hotline seems inexplicably lullish for the moment, so why not?

Kathrin, models never wear 'nighties'. They are in fact,

to a girlie, constantly wearing nighties but they would be very upset if they ever found out. I swear you to secrecy on this point. The nighties all the models are wearing should always be referred to as evening dresses. And because it has taken over all the nighties, the fashion industry has had to recommend to us a couple of other bedwear options:

1   singlet and G-string. Can be teamed with stilettos and, if you want to get catwalkie about it, a Weet-Bix box on your head and a roller skate sticking out of your navel. Very num-num. Or,

2   a perfectly enormous pair of pyjamas buttoned right up to the neck, with cuffs flapping below the hands and feet and trailing along the floor. This is

because designers now make 'one size fits all' pyjamas. And that means 'one size fits all people currently contracted to the Chicago Bulls'.

Whatever happened to the matching diaphanous negligee and brunch coat, made to match one's satin bedspread and the curtains, which should be those artfully scrunched-up, tasselly sort of arrangements? A person in that sort of outfit would feel obliged to (a) learn swooning, (b) grab the outer edge of the garments and run around on tippy toe, flapping bits as they went, singing, 'Oh, wonderful youoooooo', or (c) intermittently shriek things like 'Count Yorga the vampyre! Aieeee!'

And let us not forget the Esso-sponsored Marvellous Melbourne Midwinter Night's Dream Gas Crisis Outfit. This consists of a singlet, a spencer, a full wetsuit, one of those old blokes' dressing-gowns with the draggy cord, a balaclava, a scarf, ugh boots, earmuffs, mittens, a parka, some rat-fur underpants, a couple of hairy dogs and a tea-cosy.

(These are not things that fashion designers will be draping about their muses. Not because they are too ludicrous to wear, but because using rat fur is roolly cruel.)

You can't tell me all those celebrities actually sleep in that mustard-coloured French silk lingerie they're always photographed in. Half of it would be lost forever up famous bum cracks by the time they're into rapid eye movement. It is a sorrowful mystery that most designers are not excited by the thought of working with pink winceyette.

Kathrin, consider the following quoted comments of a fashion designer called Roy, in a magazine last week: 'I never make a mistake', 'My style is about less talk and more action' and '[my favourite garment is] a Che Guevara T-shirt: I am a big fan of politically incorrect clothing.' Now, Kathrin, admit it. You haven't got the faintest idea what he's talking about, have you? That's because the man's clearly a GENIUS. An absolute GENIUS.

You don't think people like that have got time to design something just so you can go to bed without parts of you making auto-cryogenical adjustments, do you? Good God, woman, what is the POINT of popping on something just to keep your kidneys toasty if there's nobody to applaud and say, 'Darling! They. Are. DIVINE. Now, DO come and meet Jeremy!'

And that is why there are no more nighties, only evening gowns with drool stains on them.

Casino!

Episode three

[*fade up thrilling theme music*]

ANNOUNCER: Stay tuned, listeners, for shortly it's the wildly thrilling *Foxy Ladies* radio serial, *Casino!* Sponsored by the Hoist-it Company's NEW Amazement Bra with three false nipples! Yes, coming up soon on the program, it's *Casino!* Starring:

> **Helena Handbasket** as acting has-been Joan Hack
> **Daphne Toggle** as the innocent Lizzie Goody Good
> **Jeremy Blender** as her husband, John Goody Good
> **Dame Peggy Blancmange** as the woman with a gigantic income and a bust to match, Lady Chooky Cripps
> **Barry Barrymore** as Dash Trowel, private detective

and introducing –
Dirk Colander as the maître d'.

Stay tuned for *Casino!*
[*theme music ends*]

ANNOUNCER: Last week on *Casino!* you heard Lady
Chooky Cripps say –

LADY CHOOKY CRIPPS: Get stuffed, the lot of you!

ANNOUNCER: And now we join Lizzie Goody Good
and the other *Casino!* players in the roulette
nook.

LIZZIE GOODY GOOD: Oh, Miss Hack, I don't
know what happened. One minute John was
wheeling me along the balcony, and the next
I was catapulted out of the chair and over the
balustrade! If I hadn't landed on Lady
Chooky Cripps's bosom I might have been
quite seriously injured.

LADY CHOOKY: Don't mention it, you bizarre little
creature! Waiter! Forty-seven pints of
daiquiris and half a haunch of beef, thenk
yor!

MAÎTRE D': Certainly, modom, and may I say you're
looking particularly enormous this evening.

LADY CHOOKY [*calling after the maître d'*]: And get
those trousers orf!

JOAN HACK: Lizzie, don't you think it's a little suspicious that you were with your husband when you lost your legs in Africa and tonight he tried to hurl you to your death?

LIZZIE: What can you mean, Miss Hack? John is devoted to me. I'm sure I just put my legs down somewhere for a moment in Zimbabwe and forgot all about them. Why, you're simply a bitter, desiccated, tawdry old Hollywood has-been.

JOAN: You left out 'drunken slut', honey. Well, Dash Trowel, private detective, how about a little detecting?

DASH TROWEL: Don't get wise. I hate that in a woman. Where is your husband now, Lizzie?

LIZZIE: I don't know . . . [*seductively*] Dash. What's that smell?

LADY CHOOKY: Oh, that's my scent, dear. It's called Spoor of Rhinoceros – my ninth husband bought it for me at a wiglet festival in Botswana.

LIZZIE: Oh, my God, it's all coming back . . . Africa . . . the rhino darnce . . . the throbbing, undulating, drug-addled . . . arrrghhh! [*harp noise*] Stop, thief! That poacher is running away with my legs! John!

JOHN GOODY GOOD: Don't make a fuss, Lizzie. Let's head for the casino with the housekeeping. Oh, put a Band-aid on for heaven's sake – those legs look hideously untidy.

[*dream sequence harp music*]

LIZZIE: Oh, my God, now I remember! Dash! I mean, Mr Trowel! What can I do now? I'm so helpless and frightened and blonde!

JOAN: So that's your game, Lizzie!

ANNOUNCER: Tune in to *Casino!* next week, when you'll hear Lady Chooky Cripps say –

LADY CHOOKY: Look out! It's a giant iceberg off the starboard bow! And it's nearly as large as my bust! Chop it up and stick it in a glass of whisky. I'll be on the poop deck!

[*music out*]

The financial system
kind of explained

The application to register for the new tax system (GST), which you may have received, asks some pretty impertinent questions; for example, 'Do you intend to apply for a diesel fuel rebate?' Don't rush me – I haven't decided.

'Will you sell luxury cars?' Well, if somebody leaves a daffodil-yellow Lamborghini Diablo in the letterbox, I reserve the right to pop a par in the *Trading Post*.

'Will you be involved in manufacturing, wholesaling, importing or exporting alcoholic beverages?' No. I shall be drinking them in enormous quantities just as soon as I finish filling in this hideous form.

'If your estimated annual turnover is less than $20 million, do you want to lodge your annual Business Activity Statement monthly?' Well, that's just compleeeetely hypothetical.

The form says I must tick a box to describe my 'industry'. I am not allowed to make up a box because the tax office wants to collate statistics. The closest thing is 'cultural and recreational services' – which means that writers and cartoonists will be included with orienteering holiday organisers, fireworks consultants, belly dancers, tracky-dack

NEW TAX EXPLAINED:

I'll give you $5 to stop wearing that toilet dolly on your head

There's no GST if it's a luxury toilet-roll dolly running on diesel

KAZ

drawstring-toggle designers and Dannii Minogue. That ought to help with the stats. I only wish I could be in 'personal and other services' with wiglet wranglers, drug dealers, astronomers and Shontelle who works the corner near the milk bar.

The cover of the *Guide to Registering for the New Tax System* portrays the entire range and balance of contributors to our society: three men and one woman. One bloke's in a suit, one's wearing a hat and a jumper and standing in front of sheep (so I guess he's not a florist, huh) and one's in a flanny shirt and some elaborate moustachery (possibly a member of the Packer family). Although it seems too ludicrous to be true, the only woman is neatly colouring in what seems to be a gigantic margin with a pack of twenty-four Derwents (or possibly Faber-Castells – you can't see the label). Those of you having a flashback to primary school please put your head between your knees and don't forget to breathe.

The registering guide has some handy definitions such as 'You make a creditable acquisition if you acquire a thing for a creditable purpose.' Let me explain. If you go to a church fete and buy one of those crocheted nylon dollies that go over a roll of toilet paper to completely disguise the toilet roll and beautify your home, this is a 'creditable' purpose. If you have purchased one of these dollies only to wear it on top of your head, as to a barbecue, this is a 'discreditable' purpose.

Also, GST is applicable to supplies of things, and supply includes 'to refrain from an act or to tolerate an act or situation'. To elucidate: if Imelda at work is in the habit of going around singing 'The Wiiiiind Beneath Myah Wiiiings', and you bribe Mel with two (2) Scotch Finger biscuits per day not to sing it, she is supplying something and has to give 10 (ten) per cent (%) of each Scotch Finger to Colin from Accounts (Col) who, in giving them to the fussy pigeons near the third-floor stairwell window engages in an act of 'entity input' consideration.

Many of you may also have received a letter from the chief executive officer of your bank, who is paid approximately ten trillion point zero zero three to the square power of get rooted more than us. The letter will say that there is no need to worry about any computer problems in the New Year, and that 'all of [the bank's] own banking facilities are expected to function as usual'.

Which means you will still queue up to 35 minutes at lunchtime, when there's one (1) teller to seventeen people and a mime act in the queue. The telephone 'menu' (I'll have the scampi in batter and a crème de menthe, thanks) will have nothing on it you want, especially not an option to speak to a human being.

The chief exec's kindly holiday advice – 'Please try not to carry around a large amount of cash for safety reasons' ('large amount of cash' = somewhat less than bank's annual profit) – also means that they can't cosh you with the full range of vicious bank charges if most of your money's in your board shorts.

Sexual healings, wiglet peelings:

evil feelings

Today's column is entirely given over to helping men with their sexual problems. If this is the sort of matter that offends you, one can only advise you to proceed immediately to the North Pole where the activities of the Arctic hare may give you some pause. Ladies may now leave the room. (Which rhymes with 'va va voom'.)

Please address any letters of whinge to the editor written in multicoloured ink on the back of the Form Guide. (It's usually safe to begin 'Dear Sir' in the case of executives.) You may begin, 'Why, oh why . . . ?' Presumably to get yourself in the mood, you can pop on a doublet and a neck ruff and address your remarks either from, or to, a balcony of some description.

One has assembled a little library to assist on just this occasion. One shall begin with Mr R. A. Willis, MB, BS, the author of *The Facts About Sex for Boys and Young Men*, sent in by a reader called Reginaldo and published by the Methodist Young People's Department in 1926. If anyone is in possession of Mr Willis's companion volume, *Advice to Girls and Young Women*, please do dispatch a photocopy

Do Not Lie iN Bed AfteR You ARe awake...

hither. (Incidentally, Great-aunty Esmé wants to know how to find out the name of an archdeacon in north-west Western Australia in 1937. He sat next to her at a dinner that year and said he'd been on the *Titanic*.) What? Oh yes, Mr R. A. Willis.

Leaving aside his diverting sketch of female anatomy in which the bowel appears as a hearing trumpet and the ovary (singular) resembles nothing so much as a table-tennis bat, and his exciting theory that ferns, mushrooms and oysters are hatched from eggs, we pounce swiftly upon his 'impure sexual acts'. Masturbation causes nervous exhaustion and other evils unspecified: 'If you, reader, have ever indulged, much or little, in this degrading practice, STOP once and forever and you will be able to make good.' To avoid it, 'Do not lie in bed in the morning after you are awake . . . no one can stand in a cold shower and think evil thoughts.' If the shower is too severe, rub yourself down afterwards with a nailbrush.

The second immoral act one can commit is 'PROSTI-TUTION, which means sexual union with women outside of marriage.' (Mr Willis uses capital letters to great effect.)

I am indebted to an anonymous reader for a copy of *A Husband's Little Black Book of Advice* for men who do find themselves married to women, in which Robert J. Ackerman, PhD, advises 'Put the toilet seat down' and 'Pick up the kids from school.' It's so hard to remember the little things. Still, never too late to learn, although Saturday morning might be a bit late to pick up the kids from school.

And men, do not go out with anyone called Rochelle Morton, whose book *Eat Your Lonely Heart Out* ('The true story of how a mid-thirties, fun-loving non-smoker became the hottest date in town') sounds like it could have been renamed *Ay-oop, I'm a Big Pommie Tart*. But no. It is simply a paragraph review of each guy she dated (there were 700) after placing an ad in the personals (Paul ponged; Nigel, 47, lived with his mum; and Gary did a good impression of Julian Clary and Bianca from *EastEnders*, which should have set off alarm bells in nearby continents if she'd been paying attention). At the end we find out she's had a boyfriend all along. Presumably 'their' song is that one with the chorus that goes 'Maniac, maniac (something)'.

Finally, I pass on help from a *Playboy Advisor* column of 1966 to SL of Baltimore, who wrote: 'Is it proper to remove a girl's fashion wig before making love to her?' 'When making love on relatively formal (black tie) occasions, leave your partner wigged. At any time before five untressing is permissable.' One must disagree. If wiglets are not removed, you will be convinced upon awakening that you are under attack by somnambulistic, dishevelled marmosets.

Although this could help you to get up and into a cold shower before anything evil happens.

Take those poor, huddled masses . . .

and whack them again

The public dunnies round here are pretty reliable, if you like stainless-steel toilet bowls, syringes, a huddled citizen in various stages of sprightliness ranging from vomiting to dead (and pretty much bypassing vivacity), a kicked-out blue light originally installed to hinder people looking for veins, and a tap that can neither be turned off nor produce a usable flow. (This equal yet opposite effect is one of the cornerstones of modern physics.)

So imagine my spraunciness when I went to a flash restaurant recently and the Ladies' Room was equipped with mood lighting, waffled hand towels, an armchair, individually wrapped mints in a bowl, an enormous jar of mysterious cotton-wool balls and a perpetually plasticated toilet seat – when you pressed a button, a new piece of plastic wrap miraculously shimmied out of the wall and onto where the Buttocks of Others had been.

It occurred to the most ardent mint-pocketer that this is what life must always be like for the Removed. You know, that generation of politicians who were removed from real life years ago and have lost touch with their families and

friends. (Don't feel sorry for them. They got an education. Plus, they wanted to go.) But what must life be like for the Removed? Always driven around by someone else, only seeing people frocked up to Meet the Politician, they are denizens of dunnies with double-ply paper and regular cleaning. John Howard's been doing it since 1974. Phil Ruddock's been lost to us since 1973.

Oh, you know P. Ruddock – the guy who always comes third in the open heats of the gleefully smug 'I've got a bigger cream bun than you' facial expression comp in federal parliament (undefeated champ S. Crean, runner-up P. Costello). Anyway, P. Ruddock's the minister for immigration who recently sent those Kosovo refugees who were staying with us back to somewhere quite near where they came from, without a map, a cut lunch or even a pair of Bata school shoes with a dinky compass in the heel.

Phil Ruddock's gotta be one of the Removed. Most of us out here think that if you invite some people to come and stay, you don't say farewell by driving them to the local tip and slowing down the car slightly before pushing them out. Mr Ruddock says we have done everything we can for the refugees (hey, the undercarriage of their forced-repatriation plane apparently stayed attached during take-off AND landing).

The Removed look uncomfy in casual clothes. And I once heard a former Labor senator mispronounce the word 'pizza'. Relatively few members of parliament, distracted by the children, have given their gussets a spray of Tile Bath and Basin instead of Sard Wonder Soap. How many Ministers for Other People's Pensions need to add up prices in their heads when they go shopping, and always have to stop somewhere between milk and new shoes?

What sort of toilets does John Howard go to? Did he have people shooting up heroin in his children's playground when they were little? Did he ever have to explain why a man was doing a poo under the slide? (If people are too fucked up to safely dispose of their syringes, I guess you can't expect them to lead the way with toilet training.) Some suburban supermarkets may as well update the over-aisle signs: 'Spreads, Biscuits, Soft drinks, Are ya chasin'?'

We're all sick of it, the cops must be fed up, and we need to try something new.

So until John Howard lives in a neighbourhood where he can't get money out of a Flexiteller without an emaciated pus-dribbling wreck begging for money and pretending to cry and telling that same story about leaving the baby in Shepparton that we all have off by heart now, knowing that if he collapses and has no pulse you've been advised by seasoned first-aiders not to resuscitate without a special mouth guard, which you don't have, then John Howard should just stop bossing people around about designated injecting rooms.

Because otherwise, if it hasn't already, all this could be coming soon to your front yard or a dunny near you.

BYO mint.

Review: *Pacific Banana*

This week we examine the classic Australian film *Pacific Banana*, which you can get out on video. It usually costs about 70 cents for 500 weeks. Let me set the scene by telling you it was made in 1980 and stars Graeme Blundell as a man who loses his erection when he sneezes, and is chock-a-block with women in the nuddy throwing themselves at a bloke whose name I can't remember but I'm sure he's been in *Skyways* or *The Young Doctors* or something.

Anyway, the dialogue owes a lot to *Are You Being Served?*, with some tremendous work with sentences involving the word 'pussy', and some intellectual hijinks such as telling a pilot, 'I want to see your joystick.'

Anyway, I don't quite know why it was called *Pacific Banana* because there are several titles that would have been better, such as *Nork Fest Ahoy; No, Really, Graeme Blundell IS a Sex Symbol, Honest; Women Just Want to Undress;* and *Homophobic Sexist Load of Old Bollocks.*

There is some great foxy-lady work – none of the actresses have eyebrows more than one hair wide, there's a lot of light blue eye-shadow, and in some cases they look to have fallen into a vat of Pot o' Gloss just before taking off their top and hurling themselves at the nearest biological item with sideburns.

The plot revolves around Graeme Blundell's sneezing-induced impotence problem, which is illustrated each time by the same stock shot of an airport windsock deflating. Eventually this problem is solved by a schoolgirl, who is played by an actress of approx. thirty-seven.

In one pivotal scene a priest is looking up the skirt of an air hostess who is fiddling with an overhead locker. Other highlights include the plane flying over Melbourne, then Sydney, then Melbourne again within the space of one sentence; the tour of Pacific islands being characterised by the fact that they land eight times at exactly the same airstrip with exactly the same two huts in the background; Graeme Blundell calming a middle-aged passenger by holding onto her bosoms; and some macramé chandeliers.

Dialogue highlights include when Graeme Blundell asks why one of the flight attendants stays with the nymphomaniac pilot.

'Because I'm stupid,' she replies.

There's an island called Bangatitty, there are feather earrings, there's a Benny Hill style chase in fast motion. For some reason I've never seen any of the actresses' later work: I suspect after filming this they all became lesbian separatists and got jobs that had nothing to do with the film industry.

I can't wait for the remake with Gwyneth Paltrow as the poofy narrator, Marlon Brando as Graeme Blundell and Leonardo DiCaprio as the randy pilot with a raffia wig.

Ivy's mid-year experience

Hello, it's Ivy here with gardening hints for September. Or possibly June.

I'm a little bit addled. There was a mermaid in one of my gumboots this morning and it gave me a bit of a turn. Right. This week in your garden, make sure everything is thoroughly sprayed with some sort of heavy-duty defoliant to get rid of those bloody autumn leaves. Either that or, if they're up too high, shoot them off with some sort of commando weapon. I've had a bit of a cold so I've been doing a bit of aromatherapy with 245T, a terrific chemical you don't see a lot of these days. I like to squirt it up m'nostrils with a bit of kero, but you could also use a home remedy from the garden such as sewing a lemon into the back of your pyjama bottoms so you can't lie on your back. The devil makes work for Edelweiss, Edelweiss . . .

The Bull

Episode four: PR

[The Bill *theme music*]

POLLY: Sarge, I accidentally whacked a scrubber darn the estate during an arrest this morning, Guv, Sarge, Guv.

DETECTIVE SERGEANT BURNSIDE: Arrest a new villain, Pol, so we can showcase the detecting brilliance and compassionate side of the British bobby.

POLLY: Right, Guv. Oi. 'Ere's one, nickin' videos.

CRIM: All right, I did it and 'ere's a list of me accomplices.

[*music out*]

Jealously jaded about
jewels jaunt jolt

There is nothing more worthy of support than a new independent magazine, unless it's the Red Cross or a junket to the Bahamas, so good luck to *The Eye* magazine, even though one of its editors gave me a job interview years ago without bothering to take his eyes off the telly in his office. (Imagine my not being surprised when I didn't get the job.)

But the first issue's diary of Canadian model Tara Moss, dealing with the week she launched her novel called *Fetish*, may cause some readers to think that the way Miss Moss gets her book launched is par for the course. Instead of (metaphor alert) a bogey on the first seventeen holes and then a niblick-ridden hole-in-one.

Coincidentally, I have also just had a book launched, about pregnancy, so am eager to see the similarities. Her book is a rockety read about a divinely attractive, tall Canadian model trapped in a murder mystery, who needs self-defence lessons. Mine is also only partly autobiographical – about what to do if your bosoms leak and something larger than a telephone receiver comes out of your vagina. Let us then examine the highlights of Miss Moss's launch week.

'Today, couriers dropped off 12 Collette Dinnigan dresses and several glittering Cerrone diamonds.'

Actually, I usually find that before a book launch you rarely get more than nine (9) simply divine frocks sent round to your house for you to borrow on the off chance *Who Weekly* will hurl itself out of the camellias and take a snap. Before my recent book launch fewer than four Collette Dinnigan dresses arrived by courier. Quite a lot fewer than four. All right. About four fewer than four, if you want to be crisp about it.

Obviously I also have to speak sternly to the publiciste about the dearth of duck-egg-size rubies in the post, when she calls on the landline. 'Darl,' she says. 'You've got a radio interview at 1 o'clock. Don't

say "vagina" on Mike Gibson's program, will you?' As
if. 'Just get it all out of your system beforehand,' she
urges.

*'The necklace turned out to be a little too special, it
was encrusted with emeralds and took up my whole
neck . . . I'll stick with a simple princess-cut
diamond pendant and earrings.'*

I know how she feels. Pre-launch, I frantically call
my publisher. 'What's princess-cut?' I ask. 'I think it's
when you have to get all the crusts off the sandwiches,' she opines. We call ahead to the launch pad
to make sure any diamond hors dorvs doovers diver-
dans have been through topiary.

*'My mobile rang. It was a friend warning that
a photographer had just sold photos of me and a
"mystery man" to the* Sun Herald. *I laughed and
shook my head.'*

Now that is interesting. When this happens to me, I
usually laugh and stamp my foot.

*'Emma Tom calls to say . . . she's moving house . . .
all her best clothes are in boxes and if she and
David McCormack show up, it could be scary.'*

Oh, it's always scary if that rival columnist of mine
turns up with her ludicrous singing husband from the
pop band Custard. To judge from the photographs in

Plectrum Beefcake magazine, the man is usually wearing a poop-brown nylon bodysuit. La Tomatrix, God love her, could be in anything from a PVC pressure bandage to a princess-cut 'Make Mine Paddy McGuinness' T-shirt.

But it is always good to do a bit of name dropping about your launch. Nobody famous came to mine, although if your waters had broken during the speeches you could have taken your pick of obstetricians, lactation consultants, midwives and genetic counsellors. None were wearing thumping great emerald chokers, but I think they were just a bit shy.

'The Fetish *launch went by in an exhilarating blur. Kerri-Anne and John Kennerley, Col Joye and Little Pattie all showed up.'*

'Did you invite Col Joye?' I shriek at the publiciste, who claims she was too busy counting canapes and fending off CNN, Countess Ermina di Loinfruit Pavlova and King Neptune, all of whom had demanded signed copies.

'There was a lot of handshaking, air kisses and camera flashes.'

Oh look, I've run out of room.

Feeling a bit Gregory Peckish

'Those readers who are intending to read this book as well as *Unveil the Mysteries of the Female* should take note that the contents in many parts of these two books are more or less identical . . . Nonetheless the wise reader will not be tempted to skip an apparent repeat, for although the contents can be the same, the approach is nonetheless very different, and throws much light upon the more subtle differences between male and female.'

—— Théun Mares, *The Quest for Maleness*

Why haven't I snorked onto this lurk before? Writing pretty much one book and releasing it under two separate titles! Marketeers, who's the leader of our gang?

Théun Mares, says page 5 of *The Quest for Maleness*, is a seer who lives in Cape Town with his wife, Marianne. Mr Mares's main thesis is that men have been 'completely emasculated'. (Passionately one hopes this is supposed to be metaphorical.) He wishes to restore the 'impeccable honour, the quiet dignity, the unwavering hope and the

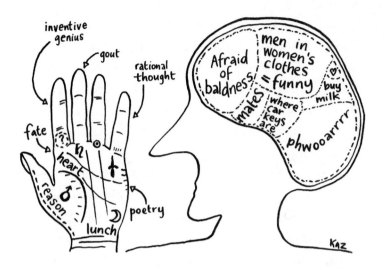

tenacious courage that is implied in the essence of the true male'.

Excellent. Get me Gregory Peck.

Instead, Mr Mares compares some natural 'void' of men with the womb: 'The womb is still, but brooding, forever ready to receive and to gather . . . the womb, until conception has taken place, is mostly passive.' Yes, or if I may put it another way, 'The penis flops about serving no particular purpose until called upon by some vessel lady.' Never mind the woman who wishes to use her womb as a menstrual-cycling venue or the chap who wouldn't mind a wee. Bugger off and find your own theory.

Mr Mares says a woman telling a man how to be a man is like a fish teaching a bird to fly, but he doesn't mind telling women how to be women, just as a dugong can explain boating to an amoeba, using rudimentary pie charts. One is not against men exploring the nature of masculinity. One is against explanations of men's creative power such as 'It is the male who carries and secretes the life-giving sperm' (not on the divan again, Craig, I've just shampooed the slipcovers) and 'The female is equally a mystery unto herself . . .'

Imagine: 'Any true act is in reality a sexual act, in that it culminates in creation.' So when two blokes work together, 'although one male cannot impregnate another male they will be able to inspire each other . . . so that each will impregnate his own inner female'. Euuuwww.

It got a bit hard there for a bit (whoopsie, sailor), but if he has a nub (ooer) I think it must be this: 'The mystery of the female can never be solved, or the potential of the female can never be realised, unless she can be incorporated into the purpose, and therefore also the life of the male.' This is done when a woman 'supports him in claiming his power'.

And now, a short dramatisation for the purposes of clarity.

Setting: Centrelink unemployment allowance queue. Enter, stage left, a long-term unempowered person and his girlfriend.

GRAHAM: Hello, I'm here for my power.
OFFICIAL: Go over there and fill in form 4 E/35367(b).
RONELLE: Just give him his power, you mongrel, there's a queue behind us going halfway to King Island.

GRAHAM: Good on you, love.

RONELLE: Don't mention it. My womb may be largely passive and I don't mind admitting I'm a complete mystery unto myself, but fair's fair.

And so we turn to *Unveil the Mysteries of the Female*, subtitled *Female or Feminist? The Challenge Facing All Women*. (God knows, it occupies all my waking seconds.) The back-cover blurb (which is about the only bit substantially different from *The Quest for Maleness*) explains that 'having proved that they can do almost anything as well as, or better than, men, more and more women are disillusioned with the empty promises of feminism'. Yeah! Feminism promised me a car! With upholstery that matched my leopard-skin outfit! Damn that feminism and its empty promises! But let him continue: 'In their search for success women have been tricked into trading a vital part of themselves for male-like qualities . . .'

So THAT'S where my appendix went.

Théun Mares, *The Quest for Maleness*, Lionheart Publishing, 1999; and *Unveil the Mysteries of the Female*, Lionheart Publishing, 1999.

It's a matter of life and death:

who cares?

Check out the cartoon on the next page. It's a puzzle that's whirring and pixilating its way through the email network and fax machines. (It doesn't come with the speech bubbles, which one has added.)

Here's the set of clues that comes with the picture: 'Shown are 4 men buried up to their necks in the ground. They cannot move so can only look forward. Between A and B is a brick wall which cannot be seen through. They know that between them are 4 hats, 2 × black and 2 × white, but they do not know which colour they are wearing. In order to avoid being shot one of them must call out to the executioner the colour of his hat. If they get it wrong, everyone will be shot. They are not allowed to talk to each other and have 10 minutes to fathom it out. After 1 minute – Q: Which one of them calls out? Q: Why is he 100 per cent certain of the colour of his hat? This is not a trick question. There are no outside influences or other ways of communicating. They cannot move and are buried in a straight line. So A and B can only see their respective sides of the brick wall, C can see B, and D can see B and C.'

Well, there are several points to make. Who cares? Why are they so badly drawn? How many human rights violations are being committed and what kind of justice is this? (Perhaps they are in the Northern Territory?)

If they're buried up to their neck, what's that weird rectangular shape that looks like an arm?

Why do puzzles always look like they were drawn by an engineering student who is surgically attached to a ruler?

Are they wearing sunscreen? Why are they all men? Is it to explain the lack of variation in the millinery?

Why are the consequences of these puzzles always so dastardly? Does this pathetic attempt to make it life or death subtly increase the pressure on us to solve the puzzle?

And why is there no picture of the executioner? Allow

me to provide an artist's impression.

Okay, I'm just stalling. I could look at the picture of the four 'men' and read the clues every day for four years and still not know the right answer. I left school so people would stop asking me questions like this. If I keep getting it sent by fax, I will have to emigrate. In my opinion, if you want something 'mind-bending', you should take some very dangerous drugs.

No sooner had people stopped sending me buried blokes than another puzzle was posed at a luncheon party: 'You have two pieces of string and a box of matches. Each string takes exactly an hour to burn, but may burn at different speeds during the hour. You have to correctly identify the passage of three-quarters of an hour, starting from now. How do you do it?'

You are not allowed to burn one string and then say, 'It was about quarter of an hour ago', because I asked. Why string and matches, why not golden thread and a Cartier lighter? And why do the strings burn more quickly at different times? What kind of string industry are you people running here?

I much prefer this email chain-letter puzzle sent to me from Queensland by my colleague Eulaliah Dumpling (Miss): 'Here's a moral question for you. This is an imaginary situation but it may be interesting deciding what you would do. You are in the outback, and there is a huge flood in progress. Many homes have been lost, water supplies compromised and infrastructure destroyed. Let's say you're a photographer out getting photographs for a news service, travelling alone, looking for particularly poignant scenes. You stumble across John Howard, who has fallen out of a helicopter and is struggling to keep from being swept away in a raging river. You must choose between rescuing him or getting a Pulitzer-prize-winning photograph of the death of a prime minister. What shutter speed would you use?'

Still, better to be trapped in a five-sided room with no door, a piece of fluff and a dumb puzzle than have anything to do with *Who Weekly*'s cover story this week: 'Body After Baby: celebs tell how they get back to work and into stunning shape in just weeks'. Because, God knows, we don't want you sleeping or breastfeeding or concentrating on your new baby. No, eat like a goldfish and get out there and do a few thousand exercises a day so you can look like Posh Spice, or possibly a balloon on a string. Because if there's anyone you can relate to at this time it's Jodie Foster or Cindy Crawford. Try and work THAT one out.

The answer to the men-in-hats puzzle is C. He realises that if D knows what colour his own hat is, and what colour B's hat is, and doesn't yell out . . . I forget the rest.

Cellulite caused by alien space rays

It's cosmetic surgery à gogo this week – the Queensland and Victorian governments are considering de-deregulating laws on ads, and a New South Wales ministerial inquiry has been hearing some horror stories. Sydney, Melbourne, Brizzie and the Gold Coast – full of the melanoma-taunting cleavages of the reluctantly ageing – are the hubs of unnecessary 'procedures'.

In Victoria four 'providers' (sounds like rows of wheat-sheaf-totin' mummas in gingham) have had eighty-nine complaints against them in ten years. Some are under investigation by the Medical Practitioners' Board, but their wheels of justice seem to move at about 0 km/h. A board spokesperson says this isn't fair: 'Some people are repeat offenders but the legislation doesn't cater for ongoing poor performance.'

Doctors accused of shoddy work or shonky ads usually come to a closed 'informal hearing' and are found not guilty or reprimanded by a board panel. An open 'formal hearing', which can result in the disbarring of a doctor, is rarer.

Only the New South Wales Health Care Complaints Commissioner has the power to bring a prosecution before the State's medical board. (The board, incidentally, has not

It's what's on the inside that counts - let's have a look inside your wallet...

Dr G.od

made any of the ninety written submissions to the inquiry.)

Victoria's Health Services Commissioner, Beth Wilson, says many of the people who came to her with complaints 'chose the practitioner . . . because they advertised aggressively.' She told the New South Wales inquiry this week that some of the complaints to her office involved mutilating scars on women's genitals.

Oh, some of these providers are just charming little self-esteem factories, aren't they? They're always on about how 'We make people feel better about themselves.' But first it helps to convince perfectly normal women they're repellent freaks with bad bosoms, stalactite-like labia and more facial lines than the average toddler, which need sandblasting.

Qualified plastic surgeons are arguing with some GPs who say they've done more laser training than the surgeons.

There's no law stopping a GP from buying a laser machine and advertising as a cosmetic surgeon. How do you regulate the shonky and the vain, the coerced and the tragic, where commerce meets 'medicine'?

The editor in chief of *Australian Cosmetic Surgery* magazine, Michelle Kearney, told the New South Wales inquiry this week that her magazine aims to give patients information, and consequently she approached doctors to write about their own activities. (So the words 'amazing', 'young', 'complete bollocks', 'breakthrough', 'quoit' and 'Pamela Anderson Lee' will be in a completely different order from, say, how I might arrange them.)

The mag warns in teeny print that some 'photographs depict models who have not necessarily received treatments described in this magazine'. (Twelve-year-old bums can't be ruled out.) Ms Kearney told the inquiry she asked doctors not to manipulate their before-and-after pictures. So, like, I guess they don't.

'If the same doctors [as those asked to write articles] wish to advertise in the magazine because they consider it a suitable environment, so be it,' she said. The ad for Doctor X's clinic will invariably be found next to an article by good ole Doc X. They write stuff about their own patients like, 'Needless to say, Sally is ecstatic with the results and finds that she has much more self-confidence than before.' Presumably then she had sex with Brad Pitt.

Cellasene herbal pills, writes a 'freelance journalist' in the latest issue, 'may finally be the miracle' cure for cellulite, 'believed to be toxins captured within the fatty areas of the body'. (And believed by some other people to be caused by alien space rays.)

The Australasian College of Dermatologists' spokesman, Dr Alan Cooper, says, 'There's absolutely no evidence of toxins in any form causing cellulite.' Elsewhere the mag says Imedeen tablets 'improve the skin's support layers by restoring collagen and elastin structure of healthy skin'. Uh, Dr Cooper? 'I don't believe it. I'd be very surprised if there was any evidence that Imedeen creates new collagen and elastin.' So surprised his eyebrows would pop off probably.

So he might enjoy the mag's photo of 'permanent make-up', which looks like a woman has rubbed off her eyebrows with sandpaper and drawn some on with an old Texta. And who could go past that divine picture of the cosmetic surgeon? He looks like a robber's dog, but it's what's inside that counts, right?

Dream date possibilities

Ladies, allow me to introduce you to Cody Lundin, a resident of Arizona who teaches survival classes. He has a licence to collect and eat animals that have been run over. He runs something called the 'aboriginal [sic] living skills school', where he teaches people to catch fish with their bare hands. He wants to live without the constraints of 'power, running water or processed foods'. He doesn't wear shoes even when it snows. He lives in a yurt but his contact lenses often freeze in their overnight solution. Contact lenses? This guy rejects all forms of modernisation (like, say, shoes) and he wears contact lenses?

And, chaps, for those of you interested in people of the lady persuasion, today's dream date is Daryl Hannah, who said recently, (a) people shouldn't assume blondes are dumb, and (b) of her recent role as a porn star, 'It was so satisfying. I never get to do roles that have as many levels as that character had. It was wonderful.'

Who Weekly magazine's best and worst dressed list

Former Sydney Swans bum-waggler Warwick Capper, a man who makes Copperart look like Ming Dynasty, comments mainly on whether he finds people attractive. Of various women he remarks 'She's got a nice sexy bottom', 'Big cleavage' and 'She's a good sort.' Why doesn't *Who Weekly* just rope in the local butcher to go 'Phwoaaarrr'?

And Tottie Goldsmith took it upon herself to remark that Christina Ricci's bosoms were too saggy. Well, staple them up a bit higher, Christina, or don't bother to leave the house. When it comes to bosoms, take it from Tottie.

Crankypants: room for ladies

I'm just a bit crankypants about trying to go to the toilet in a public place and having to decode the signs on the door. I mean, 'men' and 'women' – that was easy enough. I can even cope with those old-fashioned ones with some dude in a top hat (men) and some simpering idiot in a bonnet (women). But at a cafe the other day I was busting, and I'm confronted with two doors: one has a zucchini painted on it, the other has a drawing of a hairy pomegranate. I mean, what is going on? Vegetables can go to the toilet behind the zucchini door, and fruits can go in the other one? What about those signs where it's just a square with two legs and a small circle for a head? Sometimes that's a woman symbol, but sometimes the woman symbol is a triangle with two legs and a circle for a head because women are all sausage-shaped bald people in A-line frocks. I know I am.

Hoist-it ad

[*harp music*]

WOMAN: Slim girls, you're not very sexy, are you? You need a feather-light, roll-on Pretend Botty in modern latex from Hoist-it! Available now at all good lingerie stores.

The Bull

Episode five: budget cuts

[The Bill *theme music*]

[*sound of siren, car tyres cornering, et cetera*]

DETECTIVE INSPECTOR: Sierra Oscar, Sierra Oscar. In pursuit of a white Fiesta with a flashing blue light on top of it.

JUNE: Shut it. That's another panda car, you
        plonker.

DI: Well, it looks very small for a police vehicle,
        June.

JUNE: It's the ABC budget cuts.

[*music out*]

Memo to Stan 'Knuckles' McFeffer, literary agent, from Authoress 4576

(After it was revealed in the Victorian Parliament that an academic had been given $100,000 as an advance payment to write a book about the Kennett government and its achievements.)

Sweetie,

Please find enclosed part of the foreword to *How Grouse Was It, Ay: The Kennett Years: A Critical Appraisal* (working title). If we can't get a $100,000 advance out of someone, I'll be very much startled. Listen, I don't care what this academic bloke has already got in the can, I once had lunch with a woman from Penguin who liked my shoes, and a friend of mine used to play tongue-polo with someone from accounts in Random House, which is an encouraging name for a publishing concern if ever I heard one.

Give me a frisson on the mobile when you've got a nibble. If there's a lull in proceedings, get Spellcheck to change every ref from 'Kennett' to 'Carr' or 'Bracksy' and

have a go there. Am quite happy to work in secret, be vetted by govt officials, and if book not published will accept upwards of $50,000 or divine handbag from Louis Vuitton, as discussed. Publicity shot of me with saucepan and neighbour's labrador attached – human interest, as requested. We can say I live in Tuscany.

Ciao for now.

Moi xxxx

'Jeffrey Gibb Kennett strode across the rippling carpet of the foyer, his muscles rippling in a rippling sort of a way, stopping only to rake a reporter with his eyes, eyes like a big panthery sort of animal, eyes that missed nothing but not in an intimidating or vengeful way.

He was the Premier, fittingly meaning the first, the highest, the superior, the tippy tippy top of the heap, king of the castle, radiant leader of the first water, and yet every cell screamed humble magnificence as he shook his bonbon and reached powerfully for the microphone. Dressed by Alphonso Zaire, but without a smirkle of the usual arrogance of the well-dressed hunk who speaks to the loins of strangers everywhere, Mr Kennett brushed away a photographer hungry for a full page in his magazine's Twenty-five Most Magnetic Fascinators issue in a friendly, perky way that brooked no misunderstanding of his warm regard, and began.

One of the major problems of being possessed of an elfin and slightly transparent luminosity was that sometimes people tended not to fully engorge themselves by virtue of the majesty of his wordings. But lissom with tiny facial pores is as lissom with tiny facial pores does in the political world, and as usual Jeffrey Gibb Kennett, man of the hour, man of the decade, man of the century and beyond into the great yawning abyss of future unknowableness, delivered himself of ingenious architect-designed policies for the transformation of darkness into light, of the heaving, nasty past into shiny, skittering baubles of forward-thinking gorgeousness.

An enigma, a puzzle and a Pandora's chocolate box, with a mix of hard and soft centres and one of those ones that looks like it might have coconut in it but you can never quite identify it even when you're eating it, Jeffrey

Gibb Kennett was a man in a million with a mission. A pair of darting eyes and libidinous lips atop a lumber-carter's physique, and with the sensitivity of someone with a top-shelf soul, this man was to sculpt the community of Victoria into the vibrant, pulsing, techno-frotting maelstrom of a taxpayer-funded, sticky-carpeted, pokie-licking, multi-level, car-park-style demographic with a sprinkling of hospital beds that it is today.

And don't get me started on the hair.

This sultry child–man – who could find time to consult widely with all manner of community groups, drink eight glasses of water a day, tend to the needs of his "temple" with some vigorous stationary-bike work and keep whole office blocks roaring with laughter at his complicated gardening quips and mulch-based knock-knock jokes – never boasted about his undeniably penetrating foresight when it came to matters requiring any amount of penetrating foresight. Though many of his deeply attractive characteristics were ignored by a media more interested in school closures and languid ambulance dispatching, he did not hold this against them. Instead, it made him feel a manly pity, one he stoically kept hidden, along with his love of poetry, and small fluffy . . .'

PS Stan – there's more where this came from. Incidentally, any news on the Latvian rights for *Howard: What a Man, What a Man, What a Mighty Good Man* yet? – me

Casino!

Episode four

[*fade up thrilling theme music*]

ANNOUNCER: Stay tuned for *Casino!*, the exciting radio serial exclusively for *Foxy Ladies*! Sponsored by Mr Bulgo's Wonderpants for men. Starring:

>**Ronald Divot** as the announcer (Oh, that's me! Spiffing!)
>**Lydia Grimace** as the knowing yet desperate has-been Joan Hack
>**Gussie Gauntlet** as the fundamentally stupid Lizzie Goody Good
>**Gordon Luge** as John Goody Good and his evil twin, Barry (or possible Desmond)
>**Hermione Bintang** as the monolithic Lady Chooky Cripps
>**and featuring Stanley Pounce** as the troubled private dick Dash Trowel.

Stay tuned for *Casino!*

[*theme music ends*]

ANNOUNCER: Last week on *Casino!* you heard Lizzie
Goody Good say –

LIZZIE GOODY GOOD [*trying to understand*]:   So . . .
my husband had my legs sawn off in
Zimbabwe to pay off his gambling debts, and
I had amnesia about the entire affair until
tonight . . . why, when I met you, Dash.

ANNOUNCER: And now on this week's *Casino!* –

JOAN HACK: Look out, Lizzie – if you bat those
eyelashes any harder, the breeze will blow
off his toupee.

DASH TROWEL: Don't pay any attention to her.
I think you're a swell kid, Lizzie. Come on,
we'll get your wrap and your skateboard, and
we'll have a nice cup of . . . [*fade*]

JOAN: Well, Lady Chooky Cripps, I guess that just
leaves you and me.

LADY CHOOKY CRIPPS: Well in that case, Joan, we
have three options. One, a madly repressed
lesbian romp in which I keep one foot on the
floor to preserve modesty. Two, we inform
Lizzie and that detective that they're actually
brother and sister. Three, I ravish a porter in
the linen chute and you —

JOHN GOODY GOOD: Quickly! Has either of you
seen Lizzie?!!!

JOAN: You've got a nerve, John Goody Good,
asking for little wifey! You've tried to rub her
out on two different continents!

JOHN: You don't understand! My evil twin,
Desmond, has been spotted in the grinds! He
should never have been let ite of the nut hice
but apparently he escaped by impersonating
a master of disguise!

JOAN [*sceptical*]:   Oh, yeah?

JOHN: Last seen, he had disguised himself as me or
a private detective called Trowel.

LADY CHOOKY: Oh, shut up and kiss me in all my
private places! Feeling hot, hot, hot! [*Latin
music*]

JOAN: That reminds me . . . Waiter? Double that
daiquiri order and get me a ticket to Havana.

ANNOUNCER: Tune in to *Casino!* next week, when
you'll hear Lizzie Goody Good say –

LIZZIE: But, Dash! You're a . . . a . . . woman!

[*music out*]

Millionaire magazine

Previous efforts to become a millionaire having failed, I have been reduced to learning the ropes from a recent issue of *Millionaire* magazine ($21.25, a remarkably similar price to *Daylight Robbery* magazine and not dissimilar to the sum demanded by the publishers of *Sucker-Punch Monthly*).

It is clear that, despite having made simply vatfuls of money, millionaires don't know what day it is. Nor do they realise how far above sea level they are at any given time. Companies that manufacture watches have been forced by a humanitarian urge to take out full-page ads offering devices that can assist. Some watches are 'water resistant to three atmospheres'. (Like, Earth, outer space and Australia's far north.) Others have coaxial pushpieces. Or maybe pole-axed codpieces — I nodded off at one point.

Some of these watches are indistinguishable from an Eddie Irvine dashboard. The Bell and Ross chronograph, for example, like the 'Combat Command Automatic watch — the military pilot's choice', has four dials on it, a tachy-meter (sadly, this does not measure how tacky the watch looks) and the day and date. If you asked it nicely, it would

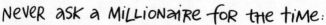

probably make you a grated-carrot sandwich.

Watches for women should carry in excess of 2000 diamonds. This makes it quite hard to tell the time during
daylight without searing your retinas, but life is not meant
to be easy. If it was, you wouldn't need a well-trained attack
dog from South Africa. Which, I feel I should be candid,
you apparently do.

Another way of checking how high you are above sea
level is to ask your pilot. There are ads in *Millionaire* for
chartering, buying or sharing 'fractional ownership' of a jet.
Or you could just check the sea level by looking out the
porthole of your 250-foot yacht, which you have cus-
tomised with 400-year-old Thai temple pillars. Or maybe
a few Chippendales (called Tad, Jut and Boff). If you're
really stuck, the *Millionaire* catalogue (those who thought

the whole magazine was a catalogue, go to your room) offers a 6-foot bronze T-Rex sculpture for $US7620. (I know all this isn't metric, but millionaires are still imperial. Boom, boom.)

There is a feature story on the suspiciously hilarious comedian Bill Murray. He and a partner own a couple of minor-league baseball teams and they have special promotions like Vasectomy Night and Lawyers' Night (when lawyers pay double to get in and then are billed each innings). There is no photographic evidence of Vasectomy Night. Bill Murray is featured as he has written a golf book and millionaires like golf clubs (logic).

Did you know that Escada, the fashion label, is totally fascinating? For example, according to the co-owner, 'A lot of people still think we're fuchsia jackets and gold buttons.' (This is at least a clue for those of us who thought Escada was a pullet-feed supplier near Horsham.) They made Jane Seymour's dress for the 1998 Emmys, which was 'created in Germany, fitted in Seymour's home in London and sent to India for beading'. That's the well-known, terribly-well-paid bead-sewers' home of India, if anyone asks.

A turret-infested 'Medieval European Manor' – with a Monet-style *jardin* – is 'offered' in Florida at $19,800,000. Anyway, you can probably get a special garage for your custom-styled Hummer armoured vehicle with soft-top or off-road hunting and ambulance package; or a double-decker bus that can be modified to accommodate a rock band or 'Mobile Launch Platform Vehicles', 'Hazardous

Waste' or 'Mammography' facilities. (Hmmm. Which look do I want: ZZ Top reunion tour meets toxic dump or *On the Buses* style missile launcher and women's health centre?)

I reached the end of *Millionaire* magazine without becoming, myself, personally, at any stage, a millionaire. But the classifieds held out some hope. I can buy a Scottish or French title and become a baronet. And to help save up, I'm going to become a lifecoach-clairvoyant and help millionaires maximise their true potential. I plan to charge by the innings.

PS If you want to get *Millionaire* magazine regularly, please contact its subscription manager, Mystie Upton.

Slavering nympho merkin-wagglers

in baseless rumours

'Some of our best-known feminists have slept their way to the top. This is true, but for defamation reasons one cannot name names except under parliamentary privilege, which I will do if the [New South Wales] Legislative Council cares to set up an inquiry into the issue.'

— Padraic McGuinness,
The Sydney Morning Herald,
4 September 1999

As usual, the florid tanklike ancient oracle is on the money. We've all heard Gloria Steinem tell a feminist barn-raising committee, 'Sorry, ladies, I'm off for a kip. Next meeting at Bella's: as usual bring a plate. Great lamingtons, Faludi.'

Of course, that paragraph is totally ludicrous. Susan Faludi wouldn't even know what a lamington was. Actually, it's just occurred to me that Mr McGuinness, that dear old venomous bag of wine-flavoured custard, may have meant that feminists have exchanged sexual favours in return for professional advancement. Quite right.

We need nothing less than a royal commission, with the following terms of reference: 'Elizabeth the Second, by the Grace of God Queen of Australia and her other realms and bits, hereby wishes her trusty and beloved judicial minion to inquire into the well-known fact that feminists are in fact a bunch of slavering, nympho, job-taking, shrewish little breast-owning merkin-wagglers.'

I, too, shall be panting to give evidence. I only wish I'd been any good at it. For years I had sex with boy reporters, only to discover that as they rose higher their postcards from Zanzibar junkets dwindled away. I considered sex with women journalists, but that seemed senseless and cruel because hardly any of them get into management. (Must be their hairstyles.)

Then a cunning plot occurred: I could sleep my way to

the top of feminism itself! As you know, feminism has a very strict hierarchy starting at the bottom with handmaidens and seraphim and going right up to Brown Owl. The main impediment to my plan to be a one-woman feminist slut-fest was that everyone else was probably doing it too.

Allow me to throw around some baseless and ludicrous allegations – it's such fun and makes me seem so important and in the know! Moira Rayner was no doubt bonking boatloads of NATO generals in a typical desperate attempt to be seconded to the Pentagon. And we've all seen the news footage of Joan Kirner on the steps of the Victorian Parliament a few years ago when she ambushed a whole raft of statisticians from the Office of Weights and Measures, gave them the full force of the Dance of the Seven Veils, stuffed the lot of them in a Triumph Herald and drove them off for a good ravishing. Who could forget how 'Oh, Put Your Pants Back ON, Joan' nearly became a national anthem?

Kerry Chikarovski? I have no evidence, but she's a woman so she's obviously a sex-crazed maniacal schemer who's had a love child with Betty Friedan. And I'm pretty sure that was Anne Summers last weekend decked out in a G-string and a pair of water wings and draped over a bit of jetty at the swishest yacht club in town. Well, someone said it was her.

I have it from a second cousin's friend of a friend that Dale Spender likes nothing better than doing the rounds of a nudey kitchen with the entire board of Microsoft. When

Quentin Bryce was in one powerful position, she found there was nobody left to seduce for advantage. Consequently, I've got a photograph of her propositioning herself behind a filing cabinet.

And as for the younger generation of feminists, they're too busy fornicating with anything that has a pulse to get anything else done. Obviously there's some sort of front organisation pretending to be involved in issues of workplace fairness, protection from violence, which articles Bettina Arndt can stick up her clacker and the issue of 'What do you want done with this pre-schooler while I'm boosting the economy, then?', while the mahogany-panelled corridors of power are cluttered with pierced clitori and confused cheerleaders.

This is because all male managers without exception are sex-enslaved ning-nongs who spend days on end appointing unqualified goers to positions of authority. I understand the next leaders of the World Bank, the International Olympic Committee and the High Court respectively will be called Candii, Jugs and the Redhead from Accounts.

Tummy Cream™

Please consider your attention thoroughly drawn to (The Original) Tummy Cream (trademark registered) (Maximum Strength) (For the Slimmer Waistline You Have Always Dreamed Of) (Abs Control) (Dramatic Breakthrough in Abdominal Cellulite Control) (Clinically Proven to Work). With so many exciting sentences, it's no wonder there's a need for all the packaging surrounding the 125-millilitre tube. Which one bought at the chemist for a weeny $38.

Tummy Cream (trademark registered) is from a company called University Medical Products Inc. in California. Which is very reassuring. I certainly wouldn't want any Kindergarten Level Pretendy Research Screamingly Expensive Gunk R Us from a company based in the Ukraine. No sirree. So, reading from the back of the box, I settled down on the couch in front of a video, ate half a black forest cake and followed the instructions to apply it to a clean stomach (that took some achieving with a scourer, I don't mind telling you): 'May be used on stomachs, obliques and lower back.' That's when things started to go terribly wrong.

It's no fault of my personal trainer, Madame Pompadour di Videoshop, but when she explained to me what obliques were, I momentarily blacked out from boredom. Involuntarily, I checked to see if my bosoms were still in position, accidentally transferring to them some Tummy Cream (trademark registered). Startled by this tragic mishap, I flailed around momentarily, and managed to get some Tummy Cream (trademark registered) on my left ear lobe, the cuffs of my culottes, both elbows, my left eyelid and shins in general. Madame Pompadour di Videoshop was slathered with it right on the dial when trying to apply an approved choke hold.

I need hardly tell you the tremendously disconcerting results. Within two to three weeks ('although results will vary'), my left ear lobe had shrunk to the size of a subatomic particle. The cuffs of my culottes had become so tight people were accusing me of wearing drawstring-hemmed cargo pantery, my elbows were AWOL, my left eye was permanently open and I could only find my shins with the aid of an electron microscope, a compass, and somebody from the Bogucki Institute. All that remained of Madame Pompadour di Videoshop's face was a stricken trace of eyebrow and somewhere to put the Tim Tams after a heavy workout of opening another bottle. Just like darling Angela from *Playschool*, she was starting to disappear for no apparent reason.

Given that the two of us had been involved in some rather vigorous lounge-room dancing and had both participated in a Mexican wave whenever George Clooney came onto the screen, imagine our horror to notice on the packaging this scarifying sentence: 'General exercise enhances results.'

It seemed that we should have read the packaging more carefully. 'Not to be used by pregnant or lactating women.' Presumably because your tummy simply disappearing entirely is not a good look in a pregnant person. And if you're lactating and you accidentally get some on your nipples in the dark, the baby will need professional help to locate the snack zone.

'Okay to be used in conjunction with female replacement therapies.' Hmmm.

'Have you ever needed a replacement woman?' Madame Pompadour di Videoshop asked idly, as she bent into a yoga position that would have had grown men moaning quietly.

'I don't think it means that,' I countered, returning the Tummy Cream (trademark registered) to a locked titanium case protected by laser alarm technology and a confused rottweiler. 'I think it means that if you were born a man but want to be another sort of person and you're taking post-op hormones, you can still use Tummy Cream (trademark registered).'

'Or,' mused Pompie, hanging upside down and refusing carbohydrates for minutes at a time, 'maybe it means that if you're on hormone replacement therapy, you may have a way higher risk of breast cancer but you can still use Tummy Cream (trademark registered) for those difficult counter-top stains.'

'That must be it,' I agreed. 'For as we have been informed, once you have gone through menopause you are no longer really female at all and must replace your feminine parts with a fairly expensive drug regime, and also get new shoes and a frock with a matching-fabric belt. Take that look off your face,' I added, as her head disappeared entirely.

How we laughed.

Parenting bullies

Are you a parent? If so, you're an incompetent, wicked, slut-tish fool who is damaging the intellectual development of your offspring. Off you pop to the local toyshop, then, for a copy of the video BabyEinstein, or BabyMozart, 'developed from research linking music therapy to an increase in spatial intelligence and physical wellbeing . . . a good head start'.

Except that watching a screen can lead to delays in brain development, according to other research. And why is there no BabyThrashMetal? Perhaps you need one of the sets of flashcards available on www.infantelligence.com to get the fruit of your loins to start memorising them.

'Ten Birds of Prey in full colour with researched infor-mation that allows you to give your baby substantial knowledge of birds of prey quickly, easily and pleasurably.' You can also, I swear, get flashcards with ten Organs of the Body; ten World Leaders, 'including Vladimir Lenin and Mahatma Gandhi'; and ten Picasso Paintings, including the bombing-aftermath memorial *Guernica* ('Look, bubba, the horse is squealing with pain and terror! You're *always* for-getting that one!').

If it isn't someone suggesting you're a crap parent so they can sell you stuff, it's someone trying to sell an article, a theory, a research institute's latest 'study' or their view of the world. All of the following assumptions come from the opinions and 'survey results' collected over the past year from Parenting Bullies reported, or reporting, in the media.

Mothers who are university-educated working women might be condemning some of their children to a statistical chance of not doing quite as many years of school as the children might have if the mothers stayed at home (but would be far less likely to be able to afford higher education for their kids); or are a danger to their children's chances of becoming a chess genius because they don't have a husband.

(Incidentally, fathers are filthy, layabout bad role models or they're at work all the time and neglect their children. But frankly, they're irrelevant. Unless they're not, in which case their sons will turn into dumb delinquents and their daughters will not even be considered worth surveying. Please don't mention single fathers or at-home dads. We don't.)

The fact that many single parents survive on very little money, managed with considerably more precision than the Defence budget, is completely irrelevant to the education of their children, few of whom are allowed in the same postcode zone as a university without visible means of paying off a mortgage. If single mothers work outside the home their kids will run amok or even, in some cases, amuk, and fail Home Ec. If single mothers stay home, they're bludgers. If they're single by choice, they're unnatural. And if they are dating, they are Glenn Close in *Fatal Attraction*.

Mothers who stay home with their children are wasting their own intellectual talents, failing to properly stimulate Mr Costello's economy, and contributing to the likely developmental delays of their children, who are not socialised by child care. Their ability to create a meal for five with $3.50 and no squid-ink croutons is a mystery to lifestyle journalists everywhere.

Parents of large families provide their children with the important socialisation of being regularly attacked and dribbled on by many other siblings, forcing them to develop strategies and recognise nuances that set them intellectually above other kids.

But kids in big families often don't get enough privacy, one-on-one attention or off-road vehicles when they turn 18, and their parents suck up too much government subsidy. They are held back by their extra responsibilities, as are the tragic lonely single children of vile, selfish parents, and the middle children of families with an L in their name who have freckles and a median household income of less than $42,000 per annum. (I'm not sure about that last bit. It was quite a small sample and my notes are smudged by caviar.)

So it is selfish for a woman to have one child, and selfish for her to have several. It goes without saying that she's completely up herself not to have any at all. For all those who are fed up with this crap by Parenting Bullies in the newspapers, I am working on a set of flashcards. Yes, there's only one. It says, 'I'm doing the best I can. Bugger off.'

One bourbon, one scotch

and one gin

As my personal necromancer and chocolate éclairvoyant, Madame Inflamer, has warned me I may soon be seeking a new career, I have retrieved the Council of Adult Education course guide catalogue from the Shoe Box of Inspiration and begun to ponder my options.

Identifying Eucalypts sounds somehow too bossy, like you'd have to stride around in large boots, with hands on hips, pointing at mystifying saplings and booming, 'That, right there, is your eucalypt.' Lose Weight Feel Great looks okay at first glance but it's certainly not as well attended as Lose Water and Muscle and Then Get Fatter Again: Feel Quite Resentful.

Commercial Coffee Making – 'Ideal for those involved in the cafe industry' (especially the ones shouting 'Look, over there!' and serving Ovaltine whenever anyone orders a skinny decaf latte) – seems a tad too specific. What's Happening to This House?, conducted by a building inspector, would be entirely superfluous. What's happening to this house is that bits are falling off it and there's a tea towel shoved in the hole in the front door to stop draughts.

♪ Shake down yo mama's holey walkin' shoes/ I done got me those Adult Education blues ♪

...do you know the Ikebana Shuffle?

BIG JOCK McWHIRTLE

Dealing With Anger, Don't Say Yes When You Want to Say No, Japanese Flower Arranging and Freeing the Writer Within are all diverting but hardly likely to lead to new, fabulously well-paid horizons.

Healthy Babies and Pre-conception Care: 'Want a healthy, happy, easygoing baby?' asks the blurb. Hands up who answered, 'No, I want a tense one who seems to scream for no reason'? But as Great-aunty Esmé always said rather enigmatically, just before she ran off with a tinker, you can have an easygoing baby or a bit of gin in the bottom of the bottle but you can't have both. May one suggest an alternative course?: Want a Healthy, Happy, Easygoing Baby? Get Up the Duff and Then Cross Your Fingers.

Public Speaking Made Easy is already in the bag. If I were running it, I'd subtitle the course Simply Drink Eight

Daiquiris and Try to Hold onto the Top Third of the Lectern. Here are some other courses that could capture the public imagination.

Bee-bothering
A precursor to the bee-keeping course. How to dress up in a nuclear-accident-style outfit, with a veiled helmet, and open up beehives. Includes stealing their honey, poking the Queen and waving your arms willy-nilly. Includes a field trip to a real hospital.

Weird Old Secretive Nuns
Discover why wizened old crones used to have the best fun hiding out in cloistery areas during the Middle Ages, writing the history of herbs and enjoying hobbies, where they wouldn't be bothered by having eighteen children and having to kiss stinking morons. What made them do it? A precursor to Hildegard of Bingen: The First Spice Girl?

Developing a Deeper Sense of Unjustified Seething Fury
You will be forced to learn how to encourage your revenge fantasies, and explore the possibilities inherent in a fully blown tantrum. Includes stamping, sulking, sneering, passive-aggressive techniques, advanced martyrdom and setting the benchmarks for unrealistic expectations.

Leaving Flowers Alone
Self-explanatory.

Getting Dumped
What to wear, where to sleep, how to whine. Features an exploration of blame, wallowing, anger, denial and bourbon. Participants will be encouraged to embark on one (1) embarrassingly inept rebound relationship during the course and may be restrained by the course tutor, Big Jock McWhirtle, from begging for sex with their ex. Some Velcro used.

Shiny Girly-girl
Take a step towards femininity with a supportive group of former manicurists. The myriad uses of glitter, cream eye shadow, depilation, the emergency application of Vaseline, crimping, simpering, giggling, putting a guy at his ease by letting him do whatever he wants, and getting the most out of a dried-up mascara will be covered in a professional atmosphere.

Finding Your Inner Bloke
Turning underpants inside out to wear the next day; why Explorer socks go with everything; one way with spaghetti bolognese; keeping coins in a jar for no reason; and how watching car racing can defuse any emotional situation. Materials needed: one slab, one Phillips head screwdriver.

Tentative Dancing

Course tutor Mitzi 'The Gal Who Put the Um in Rhumba' Fanfaronade will take you through several of the steps necessary to become a confident exotic dance performer. Each participant is expected to have partially completed a semester each of Tassel Making, Crack Walnuts with Your Own Buttocks on Stage and Booking the Light Entertainment Circuit. Call early to avoid disappointment.

Doing hokey-pokey time

Just before *Who Weekly* launches another one of those Twenty-five Most Beautifullest People Ever issues on us (usually Elle, Kylie, Paul McDermott, the usual Hollywood cull and a plump person), the *Women's Weekly* has got in first with their Worst-dressed Corporate Thieves Just Released from Pokey Ever issue, featuring A. Bond of Perth in a shirt louder than the voice of reason.

Mr Bond told the reporter that he thought Christopher Skase should have 'stayed and faced the music . . . I didn't run away, which would have been easier.' One has a vision of the tiny figure of a stoic, zeppelin-shaped patriot standing on the cliffs of Cottesloe shouting defiantly, 'Nay, I shall never turn my back and leave these shores – certainly not without my passport, which courts have consistently refused to give back to me.'

Mr Bond was in jail because in the late 1980s $1.2 billion was shooftied across from one of his companies, Bell Resources, to another one, the inventively titled Bond Corporation. This made Bond Corp look less like the desiccated, hollow-veined body of a bad actress in a negligee that the

vampires had been at, in a film based on the fall of Rome called *Friends, Countrymen, Give Me Your Life Savings.*

Eventually the jig was up, many small investors lost a lot of money, and Mr Bond went bankrupt with debts of $625 million. Which incidentally was even more than the amount of money the National Australia Bank lent him: about $600 million. (The NAB phone-banking service is now more efficient: 'Press one if you'd like to be put on hold for 25 minutes. Press two if you're a guy who missed some payments to us in the 1970s and you want approx. $600 mill.')

Here's what Mr Bond told the *Women's Weekly* reporter, who I'm sure kept a straight face, about the ethos of the 1980s: '(It) was all about how far you could push the line and I think we lost track of the fact that not only does it have to be right, it has to be seen to be right. But the lawyers told me not to worry about that.' Now either that's bare-faced gibberish or there should be a lot of lawyers in the pokey as well. Or both. And surely that's unlikely.

Readers will be horrified to learn that – you'd better park yourself in a chair for this one – while incarcerated, Mr Bond had to clean his own toilet. Furthermore, on his release, he washed up his own dinner dish in the sink. 'I had to remind Alan there is such a thing as a dishwasher,' his wife told the *Weekly*.

I would like to point out that although I was briefly a finance reporter in the 1980s I had no knowledge of Mr Bond's operations. This is largely because I had no knowledge of finance, a tradition I still maintain. Quite a lot of my time as a finance reporter in the 1980s was spent refusing to pick up the business editor's dry-cleaning and getting escorted from the stock exchange floor for being a person without a penis wearing trousers. (Women are now allowed to hide their legs at the stock exchange. Feminism gorn too far again.)

The way you reported the stock exchange was to be a cadet reporter aged approximately 16 and a half, wait until the end of the day's trading and then ring up six stock-brokers and say, 'Wassup?' or 'Have you the faintest idea if anything happened today?', and then write down what they reckoned, and then you'd put it on the front page of the business section as if the whole thing was your analysis.

It was a perfectly good system, and if some ludicrous poltroon of a journalist had stayed at lunch instead of asking

Mr Bond, 'Did you vote in the transaction to shift $1.2 billion from Bell Resources to Bond Corp?', and Bondy had replied, 'No way. Do you think I want to clean my own TOILET?', instead of something rather more affirmative, we could all still be having a nice lie down. There's always some selfish person who spoils it for everyone else, isn't there?

Undies

In the old days we had whalebone corsets and lace-up doovers and neck-to-knee girdles, and I say what's wrong with that? Obviously, if you're a woman your body shape is wrong – you'll either be too thin or too fat or too tall or you'll have some optional extras that ought to be removed, such as buttocks.

This recent story on slimming underwear in *Woman's Day* doesn't go far enough in my opinion; that is, it doesn't recommend the death penalty for women with a stomach larger than a bee's arse, and it doesn't suggest that women with breasts smaller than the Eiffel Tower should just roll around in some offal and throw themselves into a lion's cage.

There are a lot of before-and-after photos of women wearing tight undies that are supposed to hold the stomach in. As I understand it, what you're supposed to do is have your ovaries removed and get your uterus relocated to somewhere near your ear lobes; then, say you're a size 14, you pop on a pair of undies that make you look approximately the size of a starving prepubescent gymnast. Of course, when you take the undies off, you'll have a line around your midriff that they could rechannel the Murray River through for an irrigation project.

This is what's called tummy control. Tummy control is a big issue. I can't tell you how many times my tummy has just up and openly defied me, had a couple of daiquiris, gone out drinking and come home at all hours in the company of a strange shinbone and an elbow I've hardly been introduced to.

Anyway, some of these tummy control underpants you could use for catching feral cats in. They (the pants, not the feral cats) go from above the waist to halfway down your thighs, and without other clothes on you look like a cross between your granny and a demented Mormon.

I think you should probably just save your money and bandage your body so tightly you can hardly breathe and then just go around fainting a lot.

But, honestly, I've looked and looked at the before-and-after photos and I can't tell any difference except that in the after photos it appears that you show more teeth. This is either because your insides are being squeezed so tightly you can't keep your mouth closed and you're gasping for breath or you're so deliriously happy that your bosoms are pointier you just have to SING!

Also, there are some bras. I don't know what they're supposed to be for except for putting your bosoms into, but I'm willing to learn.

The Bull

Episode six: heart throb

[The Bill *theme music*]
[*sound of scuffle*]

POLLY: 'Ere. Aren't you PC Dave Quinnan?

DAVE: What's it to yer? Get in the cell, you villain.

POLLY: Well, you're the 'eart throb of the series.

DAVE: What are you goin' to do about it?

POLLY: Smack you in the gob.

[*scuffle continues*]
[*music out*]

Ads

[*harp music*]

WOMAN: Yes, girls, the Hoist-it Flatterer is here.
A long-line bra and girdle in one to provide
neck-to-knee control. Remember – if you're a
woman, your body shape is wrong! So rush in
now for your very own Flatterer. In nylon fur
or rubberised tweed.

[*New Age music, waves crashing*]

MAN [*breathy American accent*]: Kelvin Klang's Paternity.

The New Fragrance for men who can't remember
where they were the night before. Paternity.

Review: the Archbishop's message

Everyone around the country may not have been alerted to
an important message from the Catholic Archbishop of
Melbourne, His Grace from Merrily Up on High, Lord
of All He Sees Fit to Go on About, a man in a frock, a man,
Archbishop George Pell, who has been banging on all
week about the dangers of contraception, which has
caused the downfall of civilisation.

That's right: contraception is very, very bad. At this
stage I could have had about fourteen children – one a year
or so from the time I was, myself, 14 would have been a
decent sort of a contribution.

The Pill, in fact, has caused single mothers. And people
are not as happy as they used to be.

And I think the Archbishop has got it right. Because let's
look at the statistics.

Since women haven't had to spend forty years of their
life pregnant, they live longer and have started cluttering
up the streets with their shopping trolleys.

Also, since the Pill became available in Australia, more frog
species have died out, there have been several more droughts
and an increase in skin cancers.

That's our advice, anyway – listen to the Catholic Archbishop. He really knows what it's like to be a modern woman.

And, by the way, if you do have a large family and you're finding it hard to make ends meet and you're a bit weary, drop the kids off at the Archbishop's place for a few days and ask him for a big cheque. No doubt he'll be delighted to help out.

Complete wanker with
an egg-slide writes

A swag of lifestyle magazines (which fell on one at the newsagency) have reminded one of the perennial struggle of us all to have a pure white house with no furniture in it.

If any of one's housemates tries to bring home a book-case or chair or something equally ludicrous like a bed to sleep on, they get a swift lecture about minimalism and an antique turquoise beaded sling-back up the backside until they go to the stainless-steel precinct (formerly the kitchen), and make sea-urchin sandwiches on twelve-grain bread with a curly balsamic antelope nostril-hair surprise.

(Stainless-steel kitchens are most useful: if you have a burglary the detectives don't need a fingerprint kit.)

When you come home to your empty, all-white apartment wearing all-black clothes, you can look just like a pooncey Belgian mime act in a shipping container during Fashion Week, only fatter. (Ditto if you're a dark-skinned person – but don't expect to get your picture in a lifestyle magazine. You *clash* so with the curtains.)

Anyway, Australian *Marie Claire Lifestyle* magazine has gone FERAL and featured instead the all-pink Paris apartment of

a woman with a make-believe country on the Internet, Liz-bekistan, whose official colour is pink. (A Mr J. Howard has just declared Australia's official colour to be mission brown.)

What one adores about these mags are sentences like 'At the foot of the stairs sits a pair of satin and feather mules from Syria' and 'After you have bought some precious treasure from Tiffany and Co, keep the box and use it to store CDs.' (One went out and purchased an emerald tiara just so one had somewhere to put one's Motorhead collection.)

Marie Claire Lifestyle has a picture on the cover of a model kissing a blender. (The piker has decided against the big tonguer.) He's also snapped pretending he's cut off the top of his finger with a cleaver (hiLARious), in a come-hither pose featuring a giant haddock – and, my fave, with a colander on his head.

Living Etc: The Modern Home and Lifestyle Magazine begins its editorial with 'Christmas is much more hassle when you're a homeowner' (those fancy-free homeless people are so frightfully festive); advises that 'shag pile's back' (bollocks it is); and quotes a woman who explains, 'Our last home was very monochrome because I was brainwashed . . . Then I realised I was flamboyant and loved colour.' Yes, I know the feeling. I used to think I was a Tuscan peasant cook until I realised I was just a complete wanker with an egg-slide and some geraniums.

A pale Mistress of Minimal with an all-white apartment wins approval: 'wearing a white linen dress, with a bottle of Volvic water and a banana to hand, it's nice to see that she practises what she preaches'. Thank Christ the woman's got a banana or you'd never be able to find her.

These mags are chocker with useful lifestyle hints such as if stuff is untidy, put it away somewhere. (And if your hair's dishevelled, please ram down a colander over your ears.)

The Lifestyle Queen is of course the eponymous hero-ine of *Martha Stewart Living* magazine: the latest ish available here is for Christmas. Martha's the sort who knits her own stockings from waterlily stems, makes wrapping paper from logs and stone grinds her own range of exterior paint before a breakfast of home-twanged, quince-coddled pork-sicles in the shape of mittens and going on telly to explain stencilling the storm shutters with weeny fauna shapes cut from old husbands and how to fashion a lovely tuna fleet from a box of Fuzzy Felt before 7 a.m.

Martha, her mag reveals, had a menu card for her family Chrissie dinner, and always has a project going for the day. Last year it was a Scrabble game in which you could only use seasonally relevant words, this year it's building a scale model of a Maine village, with roof shingles made of pine-cone scales.

Next year they're all going to take crack.

Cat fight at the columnists' corral

'There are many columnists in newspapers all over the world who try to be funny; few succeed . . . Female columnists seem unable to stop talking about either their knickers or their cats, or their glass ceiling. While the knickers and what lies under them can excite the prurient interest of many males, and the belief that lifting up your skirt is a declaration of independence seems to be a popular notion of young women, this is a blind alley . . .'

— Padraic McGuinness,
The Sydney Morning Herald,
30 January 1998

I've tried. Really I have. I'd like nothing better than to please the blindingly snoggable Mr McGuinness . . . but always I return to my tremendous underpants and my beloved Burmese, Onan Fnaar-fnaar III.

And while we're on the subject of things catty, may I just take a moment, in my own girlishly hormone-driven fashion, to warn you against the gutter-typing of another

'. . . ANYTHING ELSE IS JUST SHOWING OFF'

female columnist in a rival newspaper, a Miss Emma Tom? A woman whose work bears noooo relation to mine, as any cursory glance at today's *Australian* newspaper will reveal. (Book readers need to know that Miss Tom's column printed on the same day as this one had some identical paragraphs. Spooky.)

The woman does nothing but go on about moggies, under-dunders and ceilings (and sometimes architraves and cornices, damn her eyes, which incidentally she should keep OFF Paddy McGuinness because I WANT HIM and I must HAVE HIM).

Sure, the aptly named Miss Tom pretends to be going on about motorcycles, tattoo parlours, Balinese typography and other subjects that bear little relation to pussy cats, lingerie and ceilings. She's just trying to impress

Mr McGuinness, or funny old Mr Whiskers Snorkypants as I call him.

Two can play at that game, you cheap hussy. On reading a collection of my previous columns, please be aware that 'East Timor' actually means 'Siamese cat', and 'water reticulation' should be read as 'Guess what's packed into my Cottontails, Big Boy?' Alert readers already know that 'Long-winded, predictable, right-wing, pompous arse-head wanker with no evidence and a ludicrous premise' refers to the difficulty of women in getting beyond middle management in the banking sector.

But here I must pause, firmly grasp the hem of my frock and gaily THROW IT OVER MY HEAD. You have no doubt seen many women, possibly even Emma Tom, doing this at bus stops and in elevators and hot-bread shops. Like the Masonic handshake, it's a secret nod to any other feminists, a sort of silent 'Gussets ahoy, Sisters! Carry on!'

(Hardliners pull their skirts over their heads and fasten them with a clothes peg. That's just feminism gorn too far. It's enough to flap it up once or twice in the bank queue, or throw over a hem in discussions with the boss to establish your independence. Anything else is just showing off.)

Which, sadly, brings me back to Miss Tom. Because, as such deeply relevant and fascinating men as Mr McGuinness know, women are only after one thing (apart from him). They go on about scones and children and ceilings and bloody cats and their disgusting private parts (which some men – go figure – find attractive!). But really they just want to scratch each other's eyes out at the merest hint of rivalry. Take Emma Tom. Please.

Just because she was around here the other day for a cup of tea, don't think I don't tire of her always banging on about her Tigger's third prize in the Large, Fluffy But Dim category at the Pussies–Galah Pet Show in Lismore. And did she even TRY to look interested when I showed her my new aqua-go-green shantung knickers just covering my blind alley? Not likely, the selfish cow – always going on about transparent room lids, when she's not getting Mr McGuinness's name tattooed on her perineum by a kitten on a Kawasaki.

Mr McGuinness is so right. Women are not funny or interesting. If I didn't have my underpants and his opinions to look forward to, I doubt I could go on. And I've got one last message for that nympho Emma Tom, who for all I know is openly using her column this week to snare the quivering-jowled god I crave. To paraphrase Ripley in *Aliens*, 'Get away from him, you bitch!'

The Queen Mother

Knowing my luck with early deadlines, by the time this gets printed in Mboko, the Queen Mother will probably have been killed in a hideous paranormal experiment involving a lady-in-waiting, a ouija board and a case of Tanqueray.

Yes, by the time this comes out, the bunting will be up, the accolades bunged on and the stilettos out for the under-ribs of anyone who dares to suggest that she wasn't godlike in her magnificence. So, in case she has in fact carked it in the last few days, please exchange any suggestion that she's simply got seniority in a bunch of rich maniacs for the respectful sentence 'Her gracious smiles will be remembered fondly, even by people on other planets, for trillions of years to come.' Ta.

Next month the Queen Mother has yet another birthday. She's kept alive by a simply marvellous constitution (not ours, hers), the preserving properties of gin and the best that medical science and a lifetime of obscene pampering have to offer. Newspapers are currently excerpting great swathes of turgid, fawning burblepoop from a book

about her by Graham Turner to which I'm indebted for the quotes that follow.

The Queen Mother's overdraft is A$10 million. The other royals do nothing about it. One grinning lord was quoted as saying that 'I'd have thought you could add another nought to that!' The Queen Mother 'did not give a fig'. As one lady-in-waiting commented, 'Why should she?' If you don't know the answer to that question, no wonder you're still waiting for something.

Oh, there are frightfully amusing tales of footmen (as opposed to handmaidens) from Clarence House carting 'oceans' of alcohol and 'vast tureens of Lobster Newburg' around. Gins are consumed before meals and champagne during. One 'old friend' remembers pouring her three triple gins before her lunch with wine, and then she walked a straight line talking lucidly. Presumably she didn't have any heavy machinery to operate.

Her life is so extravagant it even has new words in it. Every year the Guild of International Toastmasters gives her a birthday present of a nebuchadnezzar of champagne. A WHAT? Yes, never mind your pissy magnum of bubbly: a nebuchadnezzar is equivalent to about 120 bottles.

The Queen Mother (singular) has a staff of thirty to forty, including three chauffeurs for six cars, five chefs (how many does it take to slice the breakfast melon?) and 'several orderlies'. And 'three liveried footmen' – that means grown blokes in fancy dress – bring in high tea for guests. Fourteen is the preferred number of luncheon guests.

This endless gushing of extravagance is applauded by supporters, who note she doesn't spend it on jewels for herself. I doubt that would be necessary. I would imagine there are forgotten nooks in Clarence House teeming with tiaras; special humidified closets bigger than our houses for endless racks of coats made of any now-endangered species you care to mention; boxes of plumage-infested hats as far as the eye can see; and hessian sacks of emeralds as big as door knobs.

What marvellous energy she has, my dears, even annually hosting Prince Charles's stalking party at Birkhall. Yes, her relatives and friends' idea of a weekend party is to go out stalking and shooting. (In any other country we could get out an intervention order.) The Queen Mother, I believe, does not personally stalk anything. Except perhaps restraint.

It is said that the Queen Mother approved of a servant (a 'servant'!) saying that Princes William and Harry would be better off with their mother dead because their parents had different ideas about life. Only sycophancy makes this ignorant cruelty 'wise', makes a filthy rich, genial person 'gracious', turns an unconfirmed alcoholic into 'the greatest living advertisement for gin', and hails an elderly, frail woman who refuses to help herself with glasses and a stick as 'astonishingly stoical'.

Well, the Queen Mother might be a decent enough old bint who likes to put people at ease, the sort who pats a child on the head nicely and gives some hikers on her property a gin and tonic. But, really, what are the other options? Strike the child repeatedly about the ears with her proffered posy? Order some orderlies (ah, hence the name) to seize and slaughter the trespassing hikers?

Review: *Shortland Street*

Under new federal government trade-pact-related laws, New Zealand television 'product' will now be classified as Australian cultural content on the telly. So it's time we checked out the Kiwi soap *Shortland Street*, currently on Foxtel. And it sometimes pops up on SBS.

To set the scene, imagine a whole lot of Kiwi actors, many of them as animated as Besser bricks, in clothes and sets obviously purchased as a job lot when *The Young Doctors* folded. For *Shortland Street* is, in fact, a clunuc. Suffice to say that this is no *Angel at My Table* or *The Piano*. It could have been mightily livened up by Harvey Keitel in the nuddy, if you ask me, although an axe-wielding Sam Neill might have been a tad unsubtle.

Here's a bit of terrific dialogue from Dr Ropata: 'I was wanting to draw your attention to these taps . . . made in Sweden.'

Someone called Stuart is trapped in a garage, handcuffed to a Morrie Minor for no apparent reason.

Cut to the obvious femme fatale of the series, who has a very eighties perm and a jacket that looks like she had fruit salad for lunch in a cement mixer. Her lines are as follows:

'Is Michael here?'

'No,' says Dr Ropata, 'he is with his wife.'

'Story of my life,' says the fruit-salad perm.

Cut to someone returning home to find her flatmate or boyfriend ironing sheets. He gets a crease in one.

This is the explosive result: 'Damn! What's wrong with me?'

'Since when did you iron sheets, anyway?'

'Since something's something drive me crazy, all right?'

Then cut to a diet-pill casualty hooked up to a couple of drips in the clunuc, one of whom – boom, boom – is her husband, who might have to go to jail but we don't know why.

Then there is some very interesting dialogue betweeen the man who irons and another woman. He has a proposition for her and she seems awfully keen.

He says, 'Do ya wanna go for a walk?'

She says, 'Dunno.'

Okay, back to the man in a singlet handcuffed to the Morrie. The crook is American and has about six lines. Accentwise, he starts in New York and ends up in Louisiana with 'You dumb tra-a-amp.'

There's more: a vet makes a house call to take the temperature of a guinea pig in a shoe box, a nurse has $200,000 under her mattress – quite common among nurses, of course – and there's some witty dialogue such as: 'They could have locked me up and thrown away the key!', 'I'll get you for this – you'll be sorry you ever met me!', 'Not so fast!' and 'He's nothing but a big girl's blouse!'

But my favourite line occurs in the coffee shop when a man on a double date gives his order before popping off for a wee. He wants a Salada.

Now if that's not a scene straight from Australian life, I don't know what is.

Where to go for

your next holiday

I was reading this article about what life was like in the African country of Malawi, which for thirty years was run by this mad dictator, Dr Hastings Kamuza Banda. To imagine Dr Banda, picture in your mind a small African man in a fez and lounge suit waving a fly whisk and wearing the kind of rectangular glasses previously confined to Fleegle in the Banana Splits. Okay.

Now, Dr Banda had made it illegal in Malawi to whistle the Simon and Garfunkel hit 'Cecilia', on punishment of death.

Also, a bloke who happened to be drinking in a bar where two German tourists threw darts at a picture of Dr Banda was tracked down and killed.

Tourism is at a fairly rudimentary stage in Malawi.

The Bull

Episode seven: drama

[The Bill *theme music*]

DETECTIVE CHIEF INSPECTOR PADDOCKS:
'Ere! Open this door!

FILTHY CRONE: 'Oo is it?

DCI PADDOCKS: It's Detective Chief Inspector Jack Paddocks, from Stun 'ill police station, Mrs Minkins.
I want to question you about some missing doilies.

FILTHY CRONE: Leave it out!

DCI PADDOCKS: Righty-ho, then.

[*music out*]

Beauty without frontiers

'Don't worry too much if you can't sleep the night before [a] date. When you are tired, your reactions are not as defensive nor your wit as sharp, and, as we all know, most men like to feel in control.'

This perfectly charming advice is from *Faking It! How to Look Like a Natural-born Beauty* by Sarah Barclay, a beauty editor at London's *Woman's Journal*.

The book is no doubt imported to Australia from England by some humanitarian organisation keen to help the ungroomed, the great unloofahed, the dis-concealed and the non-blushered.

For someone who obviously reckons blokes are control freaks who thrill to the concept of a date with a mute insomniac, Ms Barclay sure thinks we have to impress 'em. If you have had your head shaved and spiral-permed your own moustache, some chaps pressed for an opinion of the nouveau-you vogue are odds on not to have the faintest clue and to blurt, 'Um . . . oh . . . God . . . new dress?' But we must not be discouraged.

FLIRTING WITH A SURGEON:

These are my false legs

Ms Barclay's tips for skiers are a triumph of this single-mindedness. She once tore her ligaments to buggery on the slopes. She was then traumatised by 'displaying dull, grey and hairy legs to a young, handsome surgeon'. (May I share my own beauty tip for this scenario: always carry a spare pair of tibias in an ocelot-print toiletries bag.) Ms Barclay warns, 'Even if you think you will be swathed in anoraks . . . you cannot always bank on it, so depilation and moisturisation give you a little more self-respect.'

She also explains 'oxygen skin creams': 'They work on the principle that oxygen molecules are delivered into the skin via the cream, circulation then improves and cells work harder and repair more enthusiastically.' And possibly on the principle that, if you want to sell air in a jar of fat and call it oxygen cream via an ad campaign, sales then improve, the marketing department works harder to make it sound scientific and the sales staff repairs enthusiastically to the nearest pub.

Ms Barclay explains how, when camping, you can disguise cosmetics as a painting kit, which will also give you 'an air of arty sensitivity'. Don't forget 'cheap, fake spectacles . . . will give you an air of intelligence and slight mystery'. Why not take a small child with you on a hike, to give an air of nurturing? (You can always post it home if it makes a noise.) And hey, ladies, if you carry a book, it will give you the air of kind of being able to read.

'Absailing [sic], rock climbing and all sorts of rope-and-vertical-slope-related activities are frightening', she warns, although apparently not as scary as a woman who seems to have had a full night's sleep. Does Ms Barclay suggest a good trainer who can help you gain extreme sport skills that will extinguish all but the most self-preserving fears? No, no: aromatherapy.

For travelling a 'leg spray' is suggested. Like anyone, I'm prepared to go into a chemist and order two dozen futon-sized sanitary napkins, an economy pack of Exciter condoms, a spray-on warts cure and a pamphlet on buttock fungus. But ask for a 'leg spray'? How mortifying. 'Haven't you got something that sprays into the pores and reacts with the perky molecules to dispel free-radical lymphatic toxins and makes my knees feel fizzy and look shiny, and lasts all day?'

Another great travel hint is not to bother seeing any of

the sights or enjoying the cultural exchange, but to 'pretend that you went to see a thrilling old basilica when you were actually having a relaxing massage and manicure in the nearest beauty parlour'. A real woman always skips a chance to see the Taj Mahal in favour of getting her nose pores vacuumed in a nearby cellar.

Of course, you will be wanting to know what our authoress looks like. Kindness permits me only to say (because in my own book-publicity photographs I invariably resemble a disconcerted ferret, whereas in real life I look really very much like a young and carefree Gina Lollobrigida) that Ms Barclay appears to have instead gone for a disconcerted numbat around her neck. Remember, girls: for a little more self-respect, choose furry pelt lapels! Divine! Ciao!

Sarah Barclay, *Faking It! How to Look Like a Natural-born Beauty*, Carlton Books, 1999.

Macramé versus heroin

'I say to young people, if you want to get high, go
hang gliding. Seriously, we live in a wonderful country, and while I don't want to sound like something
out of Monty Python, kids are so fortunate today.
They can go out and join a rock climbing group, they
can get a surfboard, get a hang-glider, rollerblades.
There is no limit to the adrenaline rushes they can
get, no limit to acceptable risk taking . . . sports,
crafts, the Internet, or electronics.'
— Brian Watters, the Prime Minister's chief advisor
on drugs, National Council on Drugs chairman
and Salvation Army major,
The Sunday Age, 21 February 1999

Hello, boys and girls! This week we're going to talk about
Laura Norder. Ha ha ha, just a little joke there from 1937.
No, our topic today is law and order, and I don't mean that
Yankee show on the wireless-with-pictures that has the
gravelly-voiced, short, fat district attorney who gets
wheeled in front of some leathery books every week to say

YOUNG FOLK TODAY

something like 'We don't play patty-cake with serial killers' (wise approach) or 'Cut a deal.'

Which brings me to the subject of drugs. Take Major Watters's sensible statements on drugs last weekend. Goodness gracious me, yes. What young person wouldn't choose the thrill of macramé over a lifetime of mortifying drug addiction?

Rollerblades: $100–250
Surfboard from Surf Dive and Ski: say $600
Byron Bay Hang-gliding School tandem lesson: $95
    and hang-glider: say $3000
    (you'll also need a car and petrol money to get to a
    coast – every centimetre constantly patrolled by
    Customs officers and the drug squad – or a hill, unless

you just want to hurl yourself off a Centrelink)

Indoor rock climbing all day, plus tuition and supervision
and gear, at the Hard Rock Climbing Company,
Nunawading: $14–19 for teenagers and $20–25 for
adults

Cap of heroin with up to three or four 'hits': $15–40.

I thought of Major Watters this week as a guy in a beat-up car with interstate plates crash-landed into the kerb outside our place. A young bloke slumped unconscious, doubled up like a rag doll, half in and half out of the passenger seat into the gutter. We woke him up a couple of times to ask him if he was dead. He refused a cool drink or any help and eventually disappeared after apologising politely for the inconvenience and explaining, 'I've been doing it a bit rough.'

I now realise I should have handled the situation completely differently: perhaps stood on the bonnet yelling, 'If you want to get high, embrace the romance of tatting! Have you got a Lycra crop top in the boot? I only ask because you could be ROLLERBLADING. You can probably pick up a second-hand hang-glider for under 2000 bucks! Would you like a copy of the *Trading Post*?! Wake UP!'

How puzzling that the young chappie did not seem to be seeking a high, but rather oblivion.

Another splendid advance in Laura Norder (hee, hee) is a new proposal from the Victorian government to call for expressions of interest from private organisations interested in building and running a juvenile detention centre for 17- to 20-year-old young men, with an emphasis on training and education. (And, one hopes, a spot of hang-gliding, in case they're into drugs.)

While chatting with a government spokespossum about this, I remarked that I needed some assistance in understanding what would be in it for the private company. How do you make money out of a juvenile detention centre?

'I don't know either,' said the helpful assistant, offering to go and find out.

Oh never mind. I have a much better idea. It would be far more profitable to simply sell the juvenile offenders. Once they've been convicted fair and square in the magistrates' court, we can stick 'em in the *Trading Post* and see what we get for 'em: 'Young, dangerous bloke failed and abused by parents, school, life. Thumps people a fair bit. Has shown virtually no interest in making felt hats. Potential heroin addict. Renovator's delight: perfect for hang-gliding. $75 ONO. Call Australian National Council on Drugs.'

Like Darryl Kerrigan says in the movie *The Castle*, 'Tell him he's dreamin'.'

Survival of the weirdest

A new spiral-bound book, *The Family Survival Guide: The Essential Family Organiser,* by Lucy Kelly is a boon for disorganised families – for example, there is space to list your children by name, which will cut down on embarrassing mix-ups.

There are lists of clothes to buy for the 'out of school time' wardrobe. 'Note the colours needed for individual items to help your child (or you!) put together attractive outfits based on what's already in the wardrobe.' Admittedly this is not so helpful if what is already in the wardrobe comprises only orange peel, the dog and some ancient skid marks holding together a pair of ex-Y-fronts.

One may record the details of one's holiday residential camps for children (apparently one lives in Idaho) and one's investment advisor ('I advise you to get some money from somewhere'), and ponder what the littlies will do with themselves if they are not searching for their drink bottle (there's a tick-the-box list of things to go in the lunch box).

There are *Family Survival Guide* tick-the-box lists for books recommended and read (fiction for adults, non-fiction for

adults, self-help), and party requirements (sprinkles, specify appropriate clothing if necessary, art project, video camera). There is also a list for adult parties (entree plates, artificial sweetener, napkin holders and 'enjoy'). Excuse a wee quibblette but it might be more useful to have a couple of tick boxes for 'bucket with sawdust', 'Barry's tape of *Whoa, Black Betty, Bam-ba-Lam*' and 'contact number for SAS squad'.

The 'Family Entertainment' contact list starts alphabetically at Art Galleries and moves at a fairly blindingly cracking pace directly to Bottle Shop: family entertainment my hairy grenache.

One was overjoyed to find a whole page on which to list what's in one's safety deposit box, with tick boxes galore, including for share certificates, jewellery, stamps, coins, requests for pallbearers (and instructions for which newspapers to post death announcements in, in case your family was thinking of notifying *Greyhound Weekly*).

There is space to record your brand of eye shadow, the breeding details of your pet and things to take when travelling, including a 'stool softener'. (Good idea. It can get pretty uncomfortable in some of those bars late at night.) Also – and I checked that I wasn't hallucinating – there's a section called 'If a Child Goes Missing', and you're to paste in photos of your children and change them every six months up to age 3, then once a year, and record their race, blood type, Medicare number and the names of 'police officers/other officials' you have spoken with.

Then there is the section devoted to finding a nanny or babysitter. You may tick responsibilities that include 'unstructured play' and ideal characteristics such as 'strict' and 'humorous'. Questions to ask at the interview include 'Can you legally work in this country?', 'How does this job fit with your overall career plan?' ('I intend to privatise the children and buy a brothel') and 'Do you have any medical issues I should know about?' – this is less blunt than 'Do you shoot up much battery acid to speak of?' (Ask 'Do you own a car?' on the telephone first, as this 'will end the screening interview if not answered satisfactorily'.)

One can only compare this with advice for finding a child's nurse in the 1946 Australian edition of the *Ladies' Handbook* by Eulalia S. Richards, a 1037-page book that includes a fold-out diagram of a lady's insides and a precise description of tuberculosis of the knee. The book explains that a child's nurse (presumed to be also of the lady persuasion) should possess good health, have a genuine love of little children, be conscientious, intelligent, truthful, patient, gentle and clean. (Never mind that – what about the CAR?)

Mothers should guard against an ignorant or unscrupulous nurse passing on the habit of masturbation to the children when washing them: advice still very relevant indeed today, if you are completely barking mad. Also, a nurse should not tell the children exciting stories. And if she does (let us update for the new millennium), she must keep an alphabetical list of them with a tick-the-box system recording whether the children seemed to be (a) gifted, (b) asleep or (c) producing loose stools.

Lucy Kelly, *The Family Survival Guide: The Essential Family Organiser*, 1999.

Sneak peek at

King Charles's coronation

You can't decide which way to vote on the republic by listening to J. Howard, N. Minchin, that guy singing in the 'no' ads, M. Turnbull, E. McGuire or P. Costello. Could any of them be any happier with themselves?

In case the vote goes no, we present here a glimpse of Charles's coronation-to-come. (Thanks to *Queen Elizabeth's Coronation Book*, published by the Herald and Sun News-Pictorial in 1952, for the Coronation facts and tone that follow. All references to the order of ceremony are true, except the bit about Old Kent Road.)

The sturdy yet radiantly vigorous Prince, certified as a genius by two palace physicians, shall exit the palace gates in a solid gold coach attended by footmen wearing livery to indicate their subservience to those who owe their luxury, indolence and self-importance to an accident of birth and a violent, power-drunk history. Honour shall bring pinking to the faithful cheek of the servants on this brisk day.

The pageant shall pass crowds in familiar streets: Northumberland Avenue, the Victoria Embankment and

Old Kent Road, which boasts cheap, green-plastic hotels. Those applauding may be the very offspring of those who cheered his mother, the hauntingly beautiful and wise monarch whose divine rule was all too fleeting. The crowd shall be awed, grateful and jubilant.

Inside the Abbey, the Archbishop of Canterbury shall anoint Charles's forehead with olive oil, possibly Extra Virgin, from an eagle-shaped canister with an unscrewable head, and he shall say: 'And as Solomon was anointed by King Zadok the priest and Nathan the prophet, so be you anointed, blessed and consecrated King over the people, whom the Lord your God hath given you to rule and govern.'

Charles shall clutch a jewel-encrusted sword and promise, as he promised to be faithful to his wife, to 'Do justice, stop the growth of iniquity, protect the Holy Church of God, help and defend widows and orphans, restore the things which have gone to decay and maintain the things that are restored, punish and reform what is amiss, and confirm what is in good order.'

(No monarch who promised this has ever done it, or been allowed to do it, and so instead they have mostly concentrated on the Christmas message and the racing industry.)

Peers of the realm shall be in attendance, in mantles of crimson velvet edged with squirrel fur or miniver (the winter coat of the ermine), bearing emblems of their rank in life. A marquess possesses four gold strawberry leaves alternating with four silver balls, while at least one old grunter, aka His Grace the Duke, bearing the highest rank of peerage, 'rejoices in eight strawberry leaves'. Two full yards on a train betoken a Duchess. All in all, it's a pretty Aussie sort of a vibe.

Quite near to the seated Charles shall be the Keeper of the Royal Jewel House, who oversees articles that used to be kept in a cellar with human skins nailed to the door – the skins were once believed to have been put there as 'thanksgiving for England's many deliverances from the heathen Danish sea-raiders'. In fact, King Edward the First had shrewdly ordered this end for some thieves who had plundered the jewels. Hurrah!

Four Knights of the Garter shall hold a canopy over the Royal head. The Spurs shall then be brought forth. (It is not known whether Charles will wear them or merely touch them.) He shall then sit on the Stone of Scone and don the gorgeous Imperial Mantle, embroidered with gold representing the Shamrock, the Rose, the Thistle and the Leek. The exact point of this has been entirely lost to us in the miasma of tradition.

Charles briefly shall hold the Orb, a ball of solid gold set with pearls, large rubies, emeralds and sapphires and a giant amethyst. This is the talisman of supreme political power, to signify that governments receive their executive power from the Throne. The Archbishop shall elevate Charles to 'reign with Him who is the blessed and only Potentate [God].'

The King of Australia shall then grasp the Royal Sceptre, which carries the Star of Africa, the largest cut diamond on the face of the Earth, donated by a well-known philanthropic organisation, the South African government of 1905. He also shall get crowned at some point. There is no mention of Australia, the citizens or representatives of which have no opportunity to vote for the King, their head of state by law.

'If it ain't broke, don't fix it'? Well, just how bloody broke does it have to be? Unless the polls are wrong again, it's time for Lord Relevant to dry-clean the squirrel fur and journos to brush up on King Zadok in preparation for King Charles and Not-the-Queen-But-Shut-Up-About-It Camilla. Hurrah! Now, where did we pack the Orb after last Chrissie?

Living with crazy buttocks

I would like to sincerely apologise – no, really – for not being able to bring you exclusive pictures of Drew Barrymore's buttocks in a car park. We didn't just get pipped at the post by *New Weekly*, we'd heard that Pierce Brosnan was going to waggle some glands in a supermarket so we had a couple of divisions working on that.

So, frankly, we're all exhausted. Although that could be because we're on the Jennifer Aniston diet. Which is not the current craze for the No Carbohydrate Diet (Eat Anything You Like But No Carbohydrates) as reported, but the Cardboardhydrate Diet in which you can have any amount of water as long as you combine it with cardboard. It's brilliant. Jodiii in sales has been on it three weeks and she's lost 14 kilos, and Manda from the front desk has only been on it a week and she's in intensive care.

Then there's the Barbie Thigh Diet, in which you can only eat the legs off Barbie dolls, and the Brad Pitt Diet, in which you can only eat pictures of Brad Pitt cut out from *Who Weekly* magazine and lightly sweated in a non-stick frypan. The Pamela Anderson Lee Diet used to be that you

could eat all the silicone you wanted but recently the recommendation's been cut back to smaller portions. The Robert Downey Junior Diet is a little out of most people's reach, involving as it does hard drugs and flying technicolour lizards that come out of the rear-view mirror when you least expect it.

This celebrity diet thing just will not die. The easiest way to lose weight, according to so many Hollywood stars, is to stop eating, lose your mind and hire a personal trainer to speak viciously for hours on end of possible upper arm flab at the Academy Awards. Except even Jennifer Aniston's former trainer has been quoted as saying that Jen does, come to think of it, look a bit like a twig with a wig – the new, Californian Dickie Knee – and it might be time she ate a grain of rice, or possibly struck a glancing bite at a potato or ingested an entire macarono (that's the singular of macaroni, isn't it?).

I love the way they're all still looking for the brilliant diet, as if there is one. Just when you think you've heard everything, out pops someone called something like Dr Randy Furburger, PhD, from the Cleveland Vomitorium and Reiki Clinic (appparently he couldn't get a job at the Ponds Institute). And Dr Randy will go on every show possible to say that HIS diet is REVOLUTIONARY because all people have to do is STOP EATING ROOT VEGET-ABLES from Monday to Thursday, and then eat nothing but turnips after 8 a.m. on the Friday as these will soak up all the toxins and fat cells in the body and come out as wee.

This means that if you get an A-line hairdo you can look like a Give Way sign by Christmas Eve.

Then the host will ask Dr Randy to pause right there while somebody called Tad demonstrates a machine that will exercise EVERY MUSCLE IN YOUR BODY. It is an egg-beater gaffer-taped to a treadmill with a bit of garden hose hanging off it and it costs approximately $4567 in seventeen easy payments.

Listen, if you really want to look like Jennifer, you too can drop one of the five food groups. In Hollywood, they are protein, watermelon juice, organic Chupa Chups, steamed fish, and cigars. Sure, short-term dieting eventually makes you put on weight because your metabolism is stuffed and you get stupid and tired and you'll get bad skin and your hair will look like nylon carpet and your kidneys will turn into a wizened husk and if you keep up dumb diets you'll die, but, hey, it's a small price to pay for looking like a haggard PVC pipe.

And a last word from Ricky Martin: 'I have no butt . . . It's very tiny – what can I do? Not even rock-climbing helps.' Now there's a song for our times (and Drew Barrymore): 'Living with Crazy Buttocks'. Sing it (to the tune of 'Livin' La Vida Loca')! 'They will wash away while you're dancin' in the rain/You can take your coat off and they've scarpered once again!/Outside, inside, out, we're all obsessed with buttocks!/It will wear you out, findin' our weeny buttocks/Living with crazy buttocks. Living with crazy buttocks.'

Casino!

Episode five

[*fade up thrilling theme music*]
ANNOUNCER: Stay tuned for this week's riveting episode of *Casino!*, the sizzling radio serial from *Foxy Ladies*, sponsored by *Lamingtons Monthly*. Starring:

> **Bunny Pilcher** as Clive Strange
> **Ginger Uterus** as Joan Hack
> **Lana Colostrum** as the powder-room attendant
> **Victor Lanugo** as Herr Boris, the suspicious foreign gentleman in Room Sixty-seven
> **and introducing Babs Hornbag** as Lorelei Watson the Third
> **and also featuring the Fanny and Daphne du Pont Orchestra**.

Stay tuned for *Casino!*
[*theme music ends*]

ANNOUNCER: Last week on *Casino!* you heard Lady
Chooky Cripps say –

LADY CHOOKY CRIPPS: Don't try to write me out
of this series! I'm the best bosom you've ever
had! I'm going to call my agent!

ANNOUNCER: And now on *Casino!* we join Lorelei
Watson, chanteuse, and Joan Hack, failed
actrine, in the powder room of the Starlight
Lounge.

LORELEI WATSON [*to herself*]:   I hope this clingy,
silver, low-backed, cleavage-clinging, see-
through, hot-cling-pants, clinging negligee
outfit is classy enough. [*doing voice exercises*] La
la la la la.

JOAN HACK: So you're the little party who got the
11 o'clock spot.

LORELEI: That's right, Miss Hack. Tonight I'm going to
sing 'Two Quivering Tulips Couldn't Be
Happier, Oh That You Would See, Darling'.
Do you know it?

JOAN: Only by sight, cupcake. Well, break a little
femur for me. Here, have a slug of my flask
for good luck.

LORELEI: Thanks, I *am* kinda jumpy . . . I . . . so . . .
woozy . . . uh . . .

[*thump, sound of body falling to ground*]

POWDER-ROOM ATTENDANT: That's the third
starlet you've coshed this week, Miss Hack.

I guess the 11 o'clock spot is yours again
tonight. Here, have a hand towel and a
lozenge.

ANNOUNCER: Later, in the Starlight Lounge –

RUSSIAN BORIS: Miss Hack, I am the mysterious
foreign gentleman from Room Sixty-seven.

JOAN: Oh, yeah, didn't we have sex in the lift last
week?

SEÑOR BORIS: Never mind that now. Here, take this
piece of sago pudding and guard it with your
life until you are contacted by . . .

[*Goons-like scary music crescendo, gunshot*]

JOAN: Oh, for God's sake! I have to go and sing
'Strangers in the Bath' and now there's blood
all over my swimsuit bonnet.

CLIVE STRANGE [*nastily*]:   Hello, Joan.

JOAN: Well, if it isn't Clive Strange, weenie-pants
bore and failed gambler!

CLIVE: Cut the flattery, Joan. And if you don't hand
over that treasure map, I'll tell casino
management about your little deal with the
Sheik of Onan in the penthouse suite.

JOAN: Nothing gets between me and that stage,
Strange. Not Red Hot Rhonda, not the
Channel 9 dancers. Nothing in lime-green
trousers and a Ray Martin hairstyle, that's
for sure.

ANNOUNCER [*on public address system*]:   And now,

the Starlight Lounge is proud to present
Miss Lorelei Watson, accompanied by the
du Pont Sisters Orchestra.

JOAN: Gimme that machine-gun!

[*still more terrifying music*]

ANNOUNCER: Tune in to *Casino!* next week, when
you'll hear Lorelei Watson say —

LORELEI: Joan, I . . . I . . . love you.

JOAN: There's a sequin up your nostril, honey.

[*music out*]

Makin' it easy for us to be confused

There's an ad for Mastercard that simply disgorges great gerlobs of blokey bonding as the little boy with the blond buzz cut is taken into the stands by his dad, bought a hot-dog and eventually ends up holding a priceless souvenir of the game: a glowing red cricket ball.

Only he isn't. Have another geek next time you see it and keep your eye on the ball. In the version of the ad we see, he's holding a morphed cricket ball to mask a baseball from the original American ad, I'm guessing. In the American major leagues, the baseball is kept by someone in the crowd any time it goes out of play, and if a ball in play gets even the tiniest scuff mark on it it's tossed into the stands.

Getting a cricket ball during a game here is much rarer. You'd probably have to wrestle Warney to the ground when he's popped out to think about having a durry, and go through his pockets. And for some reason the kid in the ad doesn't look Australian. It's not just the military haircut. I think it's those flawless, straight-as-an-Osmond American teeth. When Aussie kids are cast in ads, they've usually got a freckle somewhere or a hair out of place. They don't look

like they've been sprayed with lacquer and issued with four agents and a mobile home.

You can see it in a lot of the cosmetic and hair-dye ads as well. All those American women look like tall, anaemic aliens from Planet Bone Structure, with really red hair, lit by 10,000 giant fluorescent light bulbs. At least some of the US ads use grown-up people with dark skin. In Aussie ads, Aborigines are rarely there just because they're there. They're usually symbolising Essence of Outback or they're gorgeous kids doing their bit for Queensland tourism.

Not like that old postal guy in the Hallmark cards ad who looks like he's played bass guitar for Muddy Waters since 1937 and might be called Hairless Bow-legged Jefferson. You know it's one of those American ads because he starts saying something to the mum on her po'ch like 'Boy, howdie, it must be lonelier than a catfish on a craw-daddlin' skillet for th'old widder-woman yonder with that there empty mailbox.' Just as he begins to speak we cut to the face of the hauntingly beautiful single mother as the postie's lines are dubbed in for us – something like 'Strewth, poor old bint. Hasn't had a stinkin' postcard since Collingwood won a game.'

Well, okay, mostly it's just the same line with a new accent. But if 'they' can get away with it by editing and dubbing instead of hiring a whole new Australian crew for an ad 'they' will. (Apparently Joyce Mayne is actually Betsy-Jimbob Cracker from Arkansas and Dipper in the Dimmey's ad is actually played by the cranky guy from *NYPD Blue* in a wiglet.)

Anyway, it's just divine to see that Telstra is bucking this trend in its Telstra shop ad, where for no apparent reason two presumably Australian actors are talking in weirdy-sub-Brooklyn New York accents. I know Telstra works in mysterious ways, but this is even more impenetrable than usual.

I'm still getting my regular bill for 0 dollars and 0 cents from Telstra, which always says it isn't due until the next bill. Each time it arrives my intestines dance to the rhythm of 'Please, Mr Postman', fearing a real bill, but it insists: 'Service and equipment $0.00'. Best of all I love the punch-line: 'PAY YOUR TELSTRA BILL WHEN IT SUITS YOU.' Tish-boom!

The other day a friend needed a new phone connected.

Telstra said they could reveal only the date and the technician would come any time between the hours of 7 a.m. and 6 p.m. She would simply have to take a day off work, lose the pay and wait at home all day.

Perhaps some of Telstra's $3.004 billion profit (looks like a phone number, huh) might be spent on hiring someone with a scheduling skill, somebody who can ditch bills for $0.00, and a postie from the Mississippi Delta. I don't know why they'd need Hairless (Mr Bow-legged Jefferson to you), but I've never understood advertising anyway.

Hey. Y'all have a nice day.

'My Garden' by Ivy Craddock

(This article, by the *Foxy Ladies* gardening tipster Ivy Crad-
dock, was commissioned by a major newspaper, but was mys-
teriously rejected for publication.)

I live in a very attractive cottage made of asbestos fibre
and old stout bottles set in concrete, which was built for
me by some sailor friends during a party we had over a
few days at some point during World War Two. It is actually part of some crown land near the railway station. I
have lived here ever since and don't intend to change
now. Occasionally some young pup at the council tries to
tell me I don't own the land. I show them my bloomers
and shout at them that I will have my wicked way with
them if they don't leave me alone and they soon waft
away.

Luckily I have had some very nice gentlemen friends
over the years and have managed to get the water and
power on at no cost, plus a nice shed made out of old fruit
boxes and copies of the *Women's Weekly*. Roofing was a
problem until 1962 when a working bee from the local

under-19s soccer club sewed together all my old corsets and welded them into place.

Of course the facilities aren't marvellous compared with modern standards but that's all right by me. I've got a Bunsen burner, a kettle, a plastic fork and a hose, and if you can't take care of your personal hygiene on the nature strip with those items you're just not trying. I was 196 last birthday by my calculations but I may have forgotten to carry the three. I was 22 when Marie Antoinette invaded Darwin so that should give you some idea.

Right. You're here about the garden. Have some of this nice herbal tea. It's made from those angel's-trumpet trees up the back, and they've been lovingly sprayed with illegal chemicals once a week since 1973. I get them from some old pals in the airforce – they're left over from Vietnam. Some people say those angel's trumpets are poisonous but what would they know? They probably barrack for Carlton. And I know there's all this new-fangled palaver about chemicals being bad for you but it's never affected me — look out! There's a giant squid having a go at your bonnet, dear! I'll have at it with my plastic fork. Cheeky devil. I'll plant that and it will grow into a lovely camellia tree.

Where was I? Oh, the garden. Yes, I have two fruit trees that I spray every day. I've told you until I'm blue in the face, what I like to do is get in the nuddy so the spray doesn't eat into your clothes, pop on a pair of old gumboots, get up the tree and blast away for an hour or so in the mornings before the sun gets too hot. Look, lovey, I'm not sure what kind of fruit they are. To be honest with you, they haven't flowered for about six years or produced a blessed plum between them, but I think they'll come into their own this spring.

This here is a fence around the vegie garden made from an old kero tin I used to live in, and some twine from an old jumper I was knitting for the man down the road. When I found out he only had two arms, there was only one sensible thing to do – unravel the whole shebang and start again. The rude bugger. Could have told me before I exerted m'self, but that's young people for you: 86 and needs a good slapping.

In the vegetable garden here you can see lots of stakes sticking up. That stake over there is where I planted a can of pumpkin soup. That ought to be shooting up soon. Over there I planted a packet of zucchini seeds. I don't bother taking the seeds out of the packet. I just chuck an old grenade at the ground, drop the packet into the hole, and then threaten one of the council workers with my sex- ual favours until they send in a back hoe and fill in the hole. I like a sense of community, where everyone pitches in, and you don't want to get too pooncey about garden- ing, it'll give you shingles.

I do like to relax in my garden. I like to get myself onto the banana lounge on that large patch of concrete under the Hills Hoist and sunbathe in the nude. You can get some very interesting patterns from the Hills Hoist lines creat- ing saucy shadows across your body.

Another whatsit that I like to do in the garden is get out in it and shout at passers-by. At my age they say use it or lose it and I'd add abuse it. The good thing about garden shouting is there's no pressure to make any sense. You just open your gob and stuff comes out. I'm a bit like Dame Joan Sutherland in that direction.

Look, I have some very special memories of the garden over the years. There was the admiral I had in the compost heap, the RAAF navigator who I taught a thing or two about eggplants, the young sailors from Italy who used to come here and go through pints of my homemade olive oil. I could go on, but it's time to spray the letterbox.

Yes, many members of my family spend time in the garden. My Uncle Stan is over there under the pergola. He died in 1936 after a spraying incident, but I don't think the two are related. Cousins Violet and Marjorie are down near the back fence. They were having a nibble on an angel's trumpet last I saw of them, happy as Larry and quoting Shakespeare in Swahili. Haven't seen them for a while come to think of it. Eh? Oh, that would have been in the seventies I think, dear.

Of course a garden is special, you great goose. Why, in the absence of a moat, how else can you create a no-man's-land around your property in case of attack by giant rodents wearing stripey nighties and holding umbrellas? Goodness me. That's why you need one, because if you sprayed chemicals in the house every day everything would go mouldy. So that's what you need a garden for.

Yes, I do have plans for the garden. I'm thinking of volunteering it as Australia's new radioactive dump. There's no need for that Lucas Heights mob to traipse out into the desert bothering Aboriginal folk, they can just come down here with a ute and a wheelbarrow and drop the lot off. That'll teach those little aphids. I mean, there are days when I lay down some suppressive fire with bazookas and the little blighters still come back. Other than that, I'm thinking of growing crab apples for making some jam in that corner over there. What's good is that you can make glow-in-the-dark jam if you keep up the levels of DDT and wee on the lemon tree often enough.

All my spare time I spend in the garden, shouting, digging holes or drinking a bit of weed killer as the sun goes down. Moderation in all things. It's a very spiritual time, in the garden. It's just you, nature and a small air rifle a lot of the time. And of course I read newsletters people send me about various conspiracies involving migrants, UFOs and the price of 50–50 cordial. You'd be surprised how it all ties in.

I used to have neighbours. Most of them went into the compost heap eventually and the rest drifted away, just as DDT will waft over a fence. Quite poetic really. I don't miss them, to be perfectly honest. I can always shout at a passer-by if I need to.

Of course I entertain in the garden, you silly minx. I've already told you I like to sunbake in the nicky noo nar under the Hills Hoist, and if that's not a free service for low-flying helicopters I don't know what is. Every Thursday a

large horde of pixies come out of the gully trap and we have
a bit of a salon where we all tell stories. Usually they arrive
after my first cup of angel's-trumpet tea and they can stay
for hours if it's good spraying weather.

A young man with a ponytail came to visit me once –
I called him Mr Ed. He wanted to plant something that
looked a bit like tomato plants in the back. I said, 'Fill your
boots, mate!' I used to creep out at night and give them a bit
of an encouraging spray. Well, he came back in a week, rolled
the leaves up and smoked them. I said, 'Sonny, the war's over.
For heaven's sake, you should be able to afford yourself a
packet of fags.' He's under one of the fruit trees now.

Look, if you ask me my secret of gardening I'd say a
spray a day keeps nature away, and you can't have too
much concrete. If you get sick of the colour you can always
paint it again. You've got to commune with the garden and
you can only really do that if you're wearing nothing
except a pinny and some gumboots. Anything else is just
showing orf. People tell me they worry about my sprays.
Listen, I've had 44-gallon drums of this stuff out the back
since 1942 and there's only been three deaths, two explosions and a few schools closed down for testing in a downwind situation and that's not bad going. Death to insects, I
say. Never saw a ladybird I could trust: their eyes are too
close together for my liking.

When in doubt, shoot an insect with a small-bore
weapon. Gardening: it's just poetry with rubber gloves on
really, isn't it?

Man going shopping

[*shopping mall sounds*]
WOMAN: Hi, can I help you?
MAN [*surprised and terrified shriek*]: No!
[*sound of feet running away*]

[*shopping mall sounds*]
WOMAN: Can I help you, sir? I see you're looking at the Brute Trouser range.
MAN: Look, I just want a pair of strides.
WOMAN: Would you like those in brick, mint, aubergine or desert sand?
MAN: Aaaargghhhh.
[*sound of running feet*]

[*shopping mall sounds*]
WOMAN: Can I help you?
[*whimpering noises*]
WOMAN: What size are you?
[*even more whimpering noises*]
WOMAN: Did you want underpants?

[*crescendo of terrified noises, sound of feet running away*]

[*shopping mall sounds*]
WOMAN: Can I help you?
MAN: I want a shirt.
WOMAN: What kind of shirt?
MAN: One that goes on the top half of me.
WOMAN: Would you like sleeves with that?
MAN: Don't try to confuse me!
[*sound of running feet*]

Crankypants: zappy shop

Fashion often makes one a bit crankypants, I find. Donna Karan, the New York designer, has opened a new shop in Sydney that 'aims to look like a New York industrial loft'. I wonder if the sort of industrial Manhattan loft she has in mind is the sort I saw in New York, because my hotel room looked directly into several floors of a sweatshop in the garment district with little hunched women from other countries there at 6 in the morning until past 10 at night – the same people sewing and cutting.

Anyway, Donna Karan was interviewed about her new Aussie shop and said, 'I want people to get excited the minute they walk in the door.'

I was wondering how we could help – perhaps hit

people with cattle prods as they come in? A couple of hundred volts each should get them a bit excited. Or maybe they could play that song 'I'm so excited and I just can't hide it/ I'm about to lose control and I think I like it/I want you.' That might be good.

The Bull

Episode eight: friction

[*theme music*]

SERGEANT: Inspector Monroe?

INSPECTOR MONROE: Yes, Sergeant.

SGT: Ink pink, you stink.

INSP. MONROE: Yes, well. There'll always be tensions between the ranks, Sergeant.

SGT: Up your bum, with bubblegum.

INSP. MONROE: Thank you. Carry on.

[*music out*]

Bosoms ahoy

At the risk of sticking one's head into the line of ire, I'm wading into the great breastfeeding hardy-hoo. (A pause while your correspondent slips into a thermo-nuclear-strike-proof coverall with marmoset-heeled faux pony-skin shoes.)

(The big caesarean-section-versus-natural-birth fracas prompts me momentarily to speak for Those Who Have Been Caesareaned in an Unscheduled Fashion. All mums would prefer a drug-free, fleeting labour experience that goes something like 'Kum by ahhhh, my Lord, ouch. Oh, look, a baby!' How divine if a midwife's only responsibility was to drive the drinks cart on at half-time.

But when a fully trained obstetrician indicates your baby could die if labour continues, you are unlikely to say, 'Stuff that, Sparky, let's live dangerously and try lavender oil. Has anybody here been to a drumming workshop?' instead of 'Oh, all right then. Mind my pancreas.')

But back to bosoms. Mothers galore choked on their second-hand rusks when they read a headline last week saying 'Bottle Babies Asthma Risk'. In a survey of 2175

Western Australian children, it was found that the ones who were fed any formula milk at all instead of breast milk in the first four months were more likely to get asthma and allergies in childhood.

Let's get this in perspective: no cause and effect between formula and asthma has been proven. Breast milk is the way grousest thing for a baby by far: a unique concoction of mysterious growth and immune-system boosters. But giving your baby some formula before it's 4 months old will not automatically cause it to get asthma, become allergic to cheese or join a Swedish techno band. (Jolt Cola is not good for babies. That wasn't in the study – I just thought you should know.)

The author of the study, a senior research officer and nutritionist at the Institute for Child Health Research in

Perth, Ms Wendy Oddy, says if a baby is not exclusively breastfed for the first four months it's more likely to have health problems, including asthma and allergies. She was quoted in news reports as saying, 'It's very easy to go and get a bottle, but it can cause more problems in the long run.' This kind of quote makes 62 per cent of mothers want to poke researchers in the eyes with a fork.

But Ms Oddy reassured me that her study's results are not a value judgement on mothers who have given babies formula. 'We need to be focussing on mothers whose babies haven't been born yet. You need a lot of support and encouragement [to breastfeed].' (Too right. Help is available from the Nursing Mothers' Association, lactation consultants and governments that fund women's health programs. Many hospitals discharge new mothers before their first real breast milk appears, which is usually about four days after birth.)

For many women, it is not a matter of 'It's very easy to go and get a bottle.' They have frightening breast infections, or not enough milk. Not many mums give up breastfeeding so they can drink more metho and go out with sailors. And even those who have no choice tend to feel guilty, as if they're personally sabotaging their child's future health.

The devastation of formula feeding in developing countries is rarely relevant here. Most people in Australia don't mix a teaspoonful of formula with a litre of typhoid-teeming, fetid pond water if they can help it.

Children's health (and an immune system) can be improved with fresh food, fresh air, exercise and a good public health system; and in the case of asthma and allergies plenty of fish and antioxidants in the diet and a home free of smoke, carpets, doonas and hairy animals may help. Bad luck doesn't help.

There are people who were never breastfed, spent the first few years of their lives breathing in second-hand Craven-A smoke and are strangers to the wheeze. Okay, that's not a scientific result. So let's just say breastfeeding is brilliant, and we could do with more support services to encourage and sustain it when possible. In the meantime, we all do the best we can.

Now get out of my way. I've got a bottle of turps and a midshipman to meet.

Barbara Cartland: like a stadium light-tower in the wind

One trusts that all readers this morning are wearing a hot-pink armband to commemorate this week's death, at 98, of Dame Barbara Cartland, writer of *Men Are Wonderful* (among 700 or so other books), one of the last upper-class barking eccentrics of Britain and the woman who put the 'ooo' in rouge.

Who will ever forget the truly arresting image of a very elderly woman with white-blonde big hair, as much foundation, powder, electric-blue eye shadow and false eyelashes as could physically stay on, two violent circles of red rouge and flouncey frockery hung about with thousands of diamantes and jewels, which brought to mind nothing more than an especially elaborate toilet-roll dolly? (*The Times* of London's obituary tactfully described all this as 'exotically apparelled'.)

Barbara Cartland transcended parody or satire and remained oblivious to her breathtakingly bizarre appearance. Nobody bothered to run the more traditional 'young and beautiful' shots with her obituaries. Every day was a heyday. Her failing eyesight was a simple blessing: in her

mirror she saw nothing but the pink and healthy glow she claimed was maintained with honey and vitamins. (Towards the end of her life she was genuinely convinced that every wrinkle on her body had disappeared because of the cosmetics she was using.)

Long unamused by the sort of writer who whinges about how difficult it is to write (oh, go and try working on a car factory line or milking cows at 5.30 a.m.), one admires a woman for whom industrial words such as 'output' and 'production' most accurately described her regular completion of a book each fortnight. (It's doubtful they were all published, towards the end.)

Though the plots apparently bore repeating, the titles are a wonderful legacy and help to pad her listing in *Who's Who* to approximately twelve times longer than anyone else's. If only one had a copy of *You in the Home; Be Vivid, Be Vital; Be Lovely, Look Lovely;* or *The Book of Charm*. And if only, as an envious writer, one had thought of the titles that tantalisingly conjure a physical picture: *First Class, Lady?, Cupid Rides Pillion, The Audacious Adventuress, The Odious Duke, The Impetuous Duchess, The Mysterious Maidservant, Punishment of a Vixen, Love Climbs In, The Prince and the Pekinese, The Vibration of Love, Bewildered in Berlin* and *Love Strikes Satan* (ow!).

Cartland professed herself appalled by the very idea of feminism. But she divorced; had her own career for seventy-four years; organised charity pageants and the first women's motor race in England; campaigned for nurses and midwives to be paid properly; allegedly sold more than 750 million copies of her books; ran a farm; and employed staff. (And delivered mail in an aeroplane-towed glider.)

Dame Barbara described herself, rather deliciously, as an authoress. She was one of those old-fashioned English people who combines quite brutal matter-of-factness with blasts of inexplicable sentimentality. She used wonderful words such as 'impertinence', 'raffish' and 'delightful'.

She was also one of those rather bossy, tactless upper-class bangers-on who are always utterly sure of everything, keep dogs for company and remember a couple of world wars. After Princess Diana's death, she told a journalist, 'Forget the monarchy. This royal family, let's not forget, is a family of Germans. The Princess of Wales was English . . . it is she whom we will miss.' Celebrity interviewer Lyn Barber reported incredulously four years ago that she moved 'like a stoat on amphetamines', was horribly snappy and referred to her own staff as 'you dear little people'.

It is a mystery why she should have engendered so much admiration, sneaking and otherwise. I suspect that the secret included being a spectacle and quite sincerely saying mad things that other people only thought to themselves. So that even if what she said was kind of insane ('I feel sorry for the young women of today . . . grooms on horseback no longer leave notes at the door') it was invariably entertaining.

In this Hollywood-driven world of celebrities, I'd rather read what Barbara Cartland has to say about modern marriage than what Gwyneth Paltrow doesn't eat. There was nothing like the Dame. She was a great big nut case, but she was truly fascinating. Let's hope there are no optometrists where she's going.

Let bywords be your byword

The other day I was at a barbie, about 40 degrees **Celsius** in the shade, and I saw a bit of a **Casanova mesmerising** a **Marxist**. Unluckily, the post-**Keynesian Maoist** had **Victorian** values, and had also **Mama Cassed** herself with some **Earl Grey** tea and a **pasteurised pavlova sandwich**, and was in need of the **Heimlich** manoeuvre. No **Einstein**, the Casanova thought it was all an act and she deserved a **Logie**. Suddenly seeing her as **Typhoid Mary**, he adjusted his **John Thomas**, shouted 'Geronimo!' and did a **Houdini** through the **jerry-built crapper** window of a nearby dingy **Edwardian**, near **George** Street, which was a bit **Dickensian**.

All of which is a bit **Machiavellian** of me, and I must be a **judas** and betray my purpose: the above blah contains a number of references to people whose names have entered everyday language (the words in bold). I couldn't quite work out how to get in **Pap smear**, **quisling**, **gerrymander**, **teddy**, **spoonerism** or **brucellosis**.

And then someone told me that the weird oobly-oobly-wooo electronicky sound in horror space movies of the

A CASANOVa MeSMERiSeS
a MaRXiSt

1950s, before electronic synthesisers were invented (O boon to humankind), is made by an actual instrument called a **theremin** named after somebody called Léon Thérémin. It sounds like the stuff in Cornflakes that comes after niacin, I don't know how to spell it and it could be some **mickey mouse** theory, or it could be a complete **furphy**. Look, when I started this column I thought it was going to be really informative. Now I'm not even sure if Jerry Built was a person. And how I would love to put **Barbie** in the first sentence, but not even a desperate old hackette can get away with suggesting the great Australian snagfest is named after a buxom piece of extruded plastic manufactured millions of times and dressed up as a neurologist in a bikini with a fuchsia-coloured campervan. And, anyway, I think every time I write 'Barbie' I'm supposed to have a little symbol meaning trademark registered and send a small bag of South Sea pearls to the Mattel corporation.

There are quite a few extra byword names if you're in the sort of scientific caper where you measure things: **curies** of radiation (in Marie's case too many), **kelvins** of temperature and **teslas** of magnetic force. Every newborn baby skirts past its mother's pouch of **Douglas**, may be chosen for some action with **Keillands** forceps and then has its responses tested in the name of Dr Virginia **Apgar**.

But we don't have many newies. So hereby and herewith and thither and yon, may I suggest a few? If somebody is **Iggied** they are a wizened old preserved raver who by rights ought to be dead but isn't (after Iggy Pop), or perhaps **Keefed** (as in Keef Richards).

A **Reith** is a terrifying smile (as in 'He visibly Reithed and I fainted dead away'); a **Whitlam** is a wind that starts refreshing in Canberra and ends up blustering about East Timor; and a **Gareth** (Evans) is a unit of being pleased with yourself, measured in increments of **Costellos**. To do a **Mandela** is to affect a dignified defiance. And tribute to Marie Stopes, the mother of family planning, might be paid by inquiring whether a prospective sexual partner has 'Maried up' in the spirit of contraceptive readiness.

Anybody pouting, going the cleavage or making a kissy gesture when a camera goes past is **McFeasting**. Great heaving desperate dry sobbing is an attack of the **Gwyneths**, and a bad-hair day could be getting the **Anistons**. Ever since former senator Richardson's divine quotes about lying in politics, porkies could be **Richos**, as in 'I'm sure you WERE attacked by giant wart-hogs on the way home, darling, it's just that it SOUNDS like a gigantic Richo.' **Germaining** is throwing an interesting tantrum that is equal parts brilliant and nuts, as in 'When I heard he'd stood me up, I utterly Germained in the street and had to go home for a Bex.'

Politicians with integrity could be accused of **Bob Browning**, but frankly it may occur so rarely in the twenty-first century the term will die out. An apparent omnipresence can be indicated by a phrase such as 'He's **McGuired** in several cities since Thursday' and, of course, scientifically speaking, a (Freddie) **Mercury** is a unit of satin.

A Burnie ring of fire

What's going on with small-town mayors? First some guy in Coffs Harbour is agreeing with white supremacist loonies and now the Mayor of Burnie, Tasmania, has resigned in a story that involves messages from God, jogging around a building seven times for biblical reasons, and a plan for a biblical prophecy Internet centre. (The story was broken by the local *Advocate* newspaper.)

Mr David Currie, ten years an alderman of the job-starved former wood-pulp town of Burnie, was elected mayor about four months ago. He's a former member of the fundamentalist Gospel Halls church, 'also known as the Brethren', but left years ago and worked as an orderly and eventually as a personnel manager at the old hospital in Burnie. That building is now derelict, full of asbestos, and has a price tag of about a million dollars and a potential bill of $500,000 to demolish it. (Trust me, it's relevant.)

Anyway, a couple of weeks ago Mr Currie resigned, citing disillusionment with council matters and a message from God. Huh? So I called him to get the story. The things that strike one most about Mr Currie are that he is

MAYORAL CHAINS

deeply sincere, he could leave an iron pot limbless talking about the Gospel, the Messiah and the Bible, and he's not winning any prizes for making sense.

He told me that he saw an old family friend approaching his family's shop–restaurant, the Chick Queen, as he was leaving one day. 'She was talking away to herself or the Lord or however you want to put it, "Send Mr Currie out."' The woman said she had been directed by God to ask him and his wife to tea so that she could deliver him a message from God.

'So several days later —' he began.

Whoa. Someone has a message from God and you don't rush over?

'I had quite a busy week,' said Mr Currie.

Anyway, the message was that he was no longer putting God first in his life. Three weeks later he resigned, and started telling the town through letters to the *Advocate* about his plans for turning the old hospital into a biblical prophecy and Christian centre.

'I went for a jog one night and I usually just pass [the building] and I ran around it seven times [Mr Currie explains later this is the number of times Joshua and his followers circled the walls of Jericho on the seventh day, in the Bible story]. As I went around it I was claiming this place for God . . . It sounds massive . . . It sounds crazy. I know that.'

'We could use Internet systems and telecommunications to set up a call centre, almost,' says Mr Currie. 'I'm not an expert in that, by the way . . . Deep down I know I've got to do this. It could be another building. My future lies in going out and abroad, not just Burnie . . . I'm not sure how but it's got to be done. It will involve physical travel . . . and mainland Australia.'

But he hasn't got the money to buy the building and nobody's offering. 'We'll wait on God for provision.'

But what if He does not provide? 'Well, there you go – you can't fulfil the vision,' Mr Currie said from the Chick Queen. 'It's just a building . . . the temple is not the important thing. The real value is the person of Christ.' Mr Currie chuckled. 'To this day [some] Jews would take a lot of convincing of that.' I don't think he thought he was being vicious. I don't think he was even aware of how horrible it sounds.

And doesn't the whole thing seem pretty kooky? 'It does,' he said readily.

And what does your wife think? 'She's a bit perplexed', although the scheme is not as remarkable as 'the walls of Jericho coming down, the [parting of the] Red Sea, the Resurrection'. He adds that Karl Marx wrote that all history was the history of the class struggle, but Mr Currie believes that 'All history is the history of the messianic struggle, and all prophecy is the prophecy of the messianic triumph. In other words there's a glorious future.'

Then Mr Currie started to tell me something about Matthew 16, but I really had to go.

Crankypants: rug rats

My worst-ever house guest made me very crankypants. He came from New York and turned my life into a Woody Allen film, which is painful even in the cinema. He came recommended by friends, and I let him sleep on my couch for two days.

He starts following me around, only centimetres behind, going 'You know, you Australians are incredible. You're so free, so honest, so real. How do you be real?'

As you can imagine I start getting a little weirded out, so that night I lock my bedroom door. Sure enough, about half an hour after I've gone to bed, the doorknob rattles. Then I hear this creepy rustle, rustle (no, his name wasn't Russell) – he's pushing a note under my door. Among other neurotic things, it says he *wants* to have sex with me but isn't going to, *but* could he stay another week? – he wants to learn how to be *real*.

By this stage I'm completely furious so I storm out there. I've got on a pink flannelette nightie and I look a bit like Witchiepoo.

I go, 'Who do you think you are?', and he starts crying.

So I put my arm around him and go, 'Look, sunshine, enough's enough. You can stay tonight, but off you go in the morning before I get up.'

He says, 'Well, how about sex?'

I say, 'No thank you.'

I go to bed. I lock the door.

And in the morning I'm up and I'm so relieved, it's oh, what a beautiful morning, my home is my castle. I have a shower, get dressed and walk through the lounge room on my way to the door to go to work. That's when I notice the house guest is sitting on the couch with an expectant neurotic New York smile, completely in the nuddy and with my nanna's crocheted rug folded across his lap.

One was not pleased.

Review: *Funnel Web*

This is a marvellous book. Splendid Australian literature in the rarely attempted sex-crazed, radioactive giant-spider genre.

The Plot: American nuclear submarine leaks, causing beachcombing funnel webs to become nutty. The spiders get furious at humans for having sex at a party, and one funnel web runs across the patio, skitter, skitter, and leaps from ground level to head height and 'pumped every drop of venom' into a woman identified only as 'silicone-breasted blonde'.

The spider then behaves somewhat like a European soccer fan: 'He strutted and postured and posed in grim celebration. Then, in a hideous reflex, his genitals throbbed and discharged and he was overcome by an urge to descend into the earth and copulate.'

Well.

From then on it just gets better and better. There's a suggestion that spiders are actually from outer space and the book has maps of the Sydney area, which just adds to the realism as the marauding, bonking-crazed toxic spiders grow about a metre every few pages and invade the city, killing a 15-year-old street kid on crack in the Cross, some refugees from Pol Pot and a lonely old woman. That's how bad *these* spidies are.

And then the funnel webs find a river of poo underneath the city. It's magnificent prose, so let's hear the author, Richard Ryan, describe it: 'They gorged on it, their appetites insatiable from the imperative of accelerated growth. And they thrived on it, and grew bigger . . . and bigger.' Now, in case you don't quite get that, a few pages on he reiterates: 'They had nourished themselves on the abundance of fecal matter which flowed to them from every part of the city.'

By this stage the monster spiders are huuuuuuuuuuuge, with legs spanning 2 metres. They rear back and impale people on their fangs, which are 'continually dribbling glutinous venom'. A standing height of 2 to 3 metres. They move faster than a man could run. Although he doesn't say whether it's Kim Beazley or Kyle Vander-Kuyp.

Anyway, by page 104 the funnel webs have taken over Central Station in Sydney, running into crowds and impaling people and 'gorging on partly liquefied cadavers'. So the army blokes get out there with flamethrowers, but the spiders' venom, 'atraxotoxin', is now so concentrated that it dissolves skin. By page 115 a giant girly funnel web is spinning people into cocoons and hanging them around the walls of the Queen Victoria shopping complex, like in *Alien*. Sydney is entirely occupied by giant, slavering spiders, many of whom have nothing to do with the Olympic games.

So a former RAAF hero decides to bomb the Warragamba Dam and flood the joint because spiders don't like water. Again, the realism is tremendous. We know the hero had flown Lincolns in Malaya, 'a variant of the Avro Lancaster as flown by the RAF themselves in the latter part of the war'. In 1971 he was flying a Republic F-105 Thunderchief in Cambodia. As you can well imagine. Anyway, it doesn't work. The spiders are still on the rampage.

The politicians decide to drop a radiation bomb, which only makes the spiders worse, but not before the funnel webs have vomited 'uncontrollably' and the contents of their intestines have poured out of them 'in jets of bloody excrement' – and then they start eating each other. The new generation of funnel webs are 'much more massively powerful with eight legs like tree trunks', spanning 8 or 9 metres, and go around ripping off roofs and chasing refugees up and down mountains, impaling and eating them and then frolicking 'in the remains of their ill-fated victims'.

SO in conclusion let me say, not only is it brilliant writing, it's quite realistic.

Richard Ryan, *Funnel Web*, Pan Australia, 1997.

The Bull

Episode nine: Spice Girls

[The Bill *theme music*]

INSPECTOR MONROE: 'Ave you been at it?

MICHELLE: Nah, I never, nothin'. I wanta brief.

INSP. MONROE: Of course you can 'ave a lawyer. In a funny sort of a way, though, Shell, we're on your side. We just want to protect the community from tossers who pinch Spice Girls Impulse perfume.

MICHELLE: Nah, yer right. I see that now. I'll shop the blagger. Tah for the cuppa tea, an' all.

[*music out*]

Ad

[*New Age music, waves crashing*]

MAN [*breathy American accent*]:   Kelvin Klang's Paternity.
For the guy who thinks condom is a French liqueur.
Paternity. Now available in a range of skin-care
products, Spakfilla and eau de cologne. Paternity.
Now available in family size.

For yea, verily, Ben-Hur was
an Aussie bleeder

Much has been made of the new movie *Gladiator* in which Russell Crowe retains his Aussie accent. This has given rise to an Australian–English co-production to remake *Ben-Hur*, starring digitally enhanced versions of original 1959 cast members Charlton Heston and Frank Thring (see your video store).

We now publish highlights of the rough cut of the new script, *Ken-Hur* (original working title 'Ken-Oath'), a movie based on inglorious Roman rule at the time of Christ. Let us say at the outset, however, that we repudiate the risible assertions of American writer Gore Vidal, who claims that some of the original *Ben-Hur* was deliberately homoerotic.

Needless to say, whatever could possibly be homoerotic about a bunch of oil-basted muscle-boys in leather netball skirts and sculpted torso-jerkins grappling with each other and looking deeply into each other's eyes while wearing strappy sandals or go-go boots is entirely beyond me.

The provisional cast includes Barbara Windsor, of *Carry On* fame, a guy who played a plumber on *Prisoner* and Cate

Blanchett as a dungeon torch ('Yet another luminously incandescent performance' – *New Idea*).

CHIPS RAFFERTY [*digitally remastered voice-over*]: When the Romans ruled Judea, they reckoned human rights were poxy, the people were held in contempt by the government, the chariot races were more than likely fixed and there was an ugly rumour that Wilson Tuckey was the minister for forestry and conservation.

BALTHAZAR [*frankincense-bearing Diver Dan from the first series of* SeaChange]: We three kings came for the birth of the Lord and, what's more, we have pressies.

MARY, MOTHER OF GOD [*Gypsy from* Home and
Away]:   If you're so wise, why didn't you
bring some clean sheets and an epidural?
We're in a stable situation here, for heaven's
sake.

[*fade*]

KEN-HUR [*Charlton Heston*]:   The chariot race shall be
screened in letterbox format, because
otherwise all the edges will be cut off and it
will just look like two guys in armchairs
who give each other dirty looks and then
start bleeding. And may I just say that it is
every American's right to own a grenade
launcher.

PONTIUS PILATE [*Frank Thring*]:   Why, you fascinating
little morsel.

TRIBUNE TREVOR [*Dick Emery*]:   Ooh, you are awful.
Charlton – you're off to be a slave.

KEN-HUR: You mongrel bastard.

[*soundtrack of Chrissie Hynde of the Pretenders singing: 'Oooh, back
on the chain, yeah, oooh, back on the chain gang'*]

[*Ken-Hur is given a drink by Jesus while on the road*]

KEN-HUR: Good on you.

[*Chrissie Hynde: 'Fur is cruel'*]

JESUS [*Russell Crowe*]:   That's not fur, it's my wig.

DISHEVELLED EXTRA [*Fiona Horne at the Logies*]:
Ooo-aaarrrr! Has anyone not seen my
bosoms yet, then?

SECOND EXTRA [*Barbara Windsor*]: 'Ere. That was my line.

EXTRA IN HORSE BLANKET [*Judy Davis*]: Grouse parts for women in this, ay. I nearly got cast as a leprous mother but my agent did her lolly.

PONTIUS PILATE: The Charlton Heston bloke saved a Roman governor in a prawn-trawling accident and comes back amongst us as a powerful man.

[*choir of angels singing: 'La la la la la'*]

CHIPS RAFFERTY [*voice-over*]: Cripes. It's a story of indifference and cruelty, of faith and love and perfect charity. It is about the triumph of human dignity and the greatest collection of comfortable menswear I have ever seen. Tribune Trevor has gorn feral but let us join him in the famous chariot race, in which he is hoofed early on, leaving Ken-Hur aka Charlton to come from behind and disappoint the bookies.

KEN-HUR [*generally overwrought*]: The victory means nowt. My mother and sister have been taken away from me! They are forced to wear horse blankets and their illnesses are not treated properly! They have been driven from their homes and are severely discriminated against!

CAESAR [*John Howard*]:   Don't be ridiculous. You're not
       even Aboriginal.

*Last scene: Jesus is carrying his own cross. He and some thieves are to
be nailed to a cross and left to die.*

BARBARA WINDSOR [*voice-over*]:   'Ere. It's come over
       all Northern Territorian.

Let pants be unconfin'd as youth and pleasure meet

(With apologies to Timothy Shy, author of *The Terror of St Trinian's*.)

'Yes, hurry in. Settle. Tiffany – put that turkey baster down, we haven't started yet. Gels, you all know why you're here. First, a bit of housekeeping. Would the gel who decorated the art room in Titian-inspired *trompe l'oeil* murals please return a call from the curator of the Louvre. Adele Brickbat from 11C has won a special prize from Berne, Switzerland, to do with explosives, about which we'll hear more at tomorrow's assembly, I'll wager. Attendance is compulsory at Saturday's unarmed combat against St Trinian's. Bus leaves 3 p.m. sharp from the tower. Mrs Crumpetbagger?'

'Thank you, Miss Horne-Bagge. Mr Wilfred, haven't you some gym mats to air? This is women's business, I'm afraid. Righty-ho. As many of you will know, the Premier of Victoria, Mr Kennett, told a group of schoolgels this week that "our women are not producing enough offspring". And further, "The average figure for every female in this country, they're only producing 1.8 children." As you

know, Philippa and Cookie have been doing their best but have only produced three between them.

'Tiffany! For heaven's sake put it away. You will note that from now on, gels, we will be referred to as "females". This is a perfectly charming term designed to recognise us as individuals with varying hopes, needs and talents. Mr Kennett wants "females" to have more "offspring" partly so the children can look after the old people. Would the gels who are volunteering to look after Mr Kennett in his old age please stay back afterwards. Yes, Belinda, I should jolly well think you will jolly well need a hockey stick.

'Now, it is a rather bracing yet incontrovertible fact, as you are all no doubt aware from Mrs Grimbladder's film evenings, that if you are to become with child you usually have to deal with some masculine version of God's intended few. I'm sorry, but there it is. Miriam, that is a very unattractive face, but as I fully concur it shall not, on this occasion, result in the usual detention. But duty calls. The vice-president of the National Family Association thinks we can stop invasions of Australia by breeding with gusto, and we ought not "get so successful in other areas, which women are now doing, that they put aside child-bearing". Yes, Miriam, it *would* be impertinent to assume she's an alien.

Tiffany, for the last time, you may perform your demonstration a little later. There is a time and place for every — oh, hell's bells. Go and see Matron. I should think the topical application of a paste of equal parts bi-carb of soda and lemon juice will do for that tunic hem. Off you go.

'And let Tiffany's experience be a beacon of warning for any gel here thinking of going off half-cocked. Where was I? Gels, it is time for us all to come to the aid of the Liberal Party. Our new slogan is "Breed, breed, breed, wearing Tweed, Tweed, Tweed", a scent available in department stores that apparently attracts the masculine article. Further details can be obtained from Miss Swivellin. Once your offspring are able to walk on their own, post them to Mr Kennett.

Those of you in 12A Politics will recall Mr Kennett refusing to endorse the right of women to breastfeed in public. You all know that here at St Bombast's one does not wait for enshrining. If at any point some of your offspring need nourishment in a public place, I suggest you recall the wild shrieking of our school motto, "Fab Fracas Nil Faintling!", and apply it directly to your bosoms.

'Of course, the appearance of parts of your bust in the vicinity of a newborn citizen is likely to inflame passers-by into an unfortunate maelstrom of carnality. So if you are carrying a tarpaulin and some crampons, and it's no trouble, do pitch a small marquee in which to secrete yourself.

'Let us lift our voices in hymn number 69, "O Fecundity! Where is Thy Stinger?", before the lesson, to be rendered this morning by 4F's interpretive dance ensemble, entitled "What Glory of the Goer Mighty". Who shall lead us but dear Miss Swivellin, who I see is at her organ yet again.'

A glimpse of Christmas Future:

away with the pixies

It's the year 2007 and we are nearing the end of the Festival of Dysfunctional Family Stress incorporating the Fringe
Festival of Merry C-------s Whether You've Got a Family
or, Well, Whatever. All polls are pointing to a gigantic
landslide win for the yes vote on the referendum question
of 'Stuff the republic, let's cancel the whole C-------s Day
shemozzle'.

Of course, we'll all have to decide which model we
want for the 25 December holiday – the Full-on Baccha-
nalia Ritual, with optional retail grotto featuring Bacchus
with kiddies on his hairy knee, or the Solemn Christian
Day of Worship, where interested parties can dress in
burlap bags and low heels and go to church. But it seems
almost all Australians agree on one thing: C-------s as is, is
Awful.

In the last few years it has become increasingly clear
that it is the season to be jolly likely to have a mental
breakdown, become addicted to prescription drugs, stay
drunk, run amok in the streets wearing nothing but one of
those barbecue aprons with the bosoms on them, or simply

sit at the wheel of your car in C-------s traffic shouting at thin air or sobbing.

'The day Uncle Fergus gave me a nylon hairnet and threw up the sliced meat that had been sitting in the sun for three hours, I decided I'd never go to a family Chris—um, seasonal function again,' says Dwayne Bingo of Figtree Pocket.

Atheists and other non-Christian persons have been involved in several riots in recent years, protesting at being sucked into the C-------s vortex, buying presents for people who couldn't be less Christian if they fed people to lions on the weekend. Psychiatrists are sorting through the horrendous aftermath of adults lying through their teeth to kiddies about Santa Claus and screaming at shop assistants that if there isn't a Pokémon Morphin' GameBoy Weeing

Pony left in the shop there could be a firebombing in the Tough Li'l Malibu Skipper Extruded Pokémon Plastic Gun Bubbles factory warehouse.

'I realise I shouldn't have stabbed her with Beelzebub Barbie,' admitted the notorious Frustrations R Us killer, Kylie-Lee Hurlen, last week. 'But I'm glad the jury took C-------s shopping into account as a mitigating factor, and I'm looking forward to being home again with the kids.'

Statistics now show that the week before C-------s, herbalists prescribe their own body weight in kava, and doctors prescribed 480,000 brain-chemistry sets this time last year. Blackmarket Mogadon, heroin and foam earplugs for that once-a-year lunch with relatives are at a premium. The defence forces have been called in to evacuate people with their shoulders up around their ears and their spines in the shape of radio waves, who are refusing to vacate the foldy-out tables of chiropractors.

Despite desperate measures by the government – an aerial spray of lavender, geranium and ylang-ylang essential oils, and a phalanx of street performers insisting that passers-by should have a 'Happy C-------s' – the number of people who say they actually do have a Happy C-------s has plunged to .00067 per cent, and almost all of those respondents sleep in pyjamas with little feet attached.

The government's street-pixie 'Be Happy For Christ's Sake' campaign has had mixed results. 'If one more of those pixies with bells on their hats comes up to me in the street, I will be forced to garotte the little bastard with its own tinsel and shove it up a pine tree,' commented one elderly shopper recently.

Historical research shows that as late as the end of the last millennium, people spent hours during C-------s lunch getting furious at relatives with whom they had nothing in common. Emotional debacles were caused as naive people expected members of their extended family to become the Brady Bunch on C-------s Day, whereas many continued to be the self-obsessed, ignorant, narrow-minded, barking mad, nasty pieces of work they had always been, except they did it in jaunty paper hats.

The Minister for More Realistic Holidays defended the government's record yesterday. 'We were the first government to ban Bing Crosby CDs,' he said. 'And let's not forget the mandatory prison sentence for bank or public transport employees who wear those Santa hats.' Late last night the minister was executed for humming 'O Come, All Ye Faithful' in a lift.

George's

I went to the new George's department store in Collins Street, Melbourne, which opened with a big faffing fanfare last week. I didn't get an invite to that bit, so I snuck in as a paying customer the next Monday.

It is the most amazing shop. It's kind of like you've gone to heaven but it's really hell, because you want everything and you can't afford it. And then you come home with all these images of shining glass and velvets and things with feathers on them, and you just think, 'I'm a bit tawdry really, living a very ordinary little life in a rather shabby little house, and I don't know why I bother.'

Okay, so let me set the scene of the first day in George's. You walk in through a bit of floristry in the foyer, and then you go up the stairs into a room full of gigantic bottles of perfume and men's shirts in different colours, all stacked like huge crayon boxes to the high ceiling.

There are hats that look like they've come straight off the scone of a New Guinea highlander, and handbags that look like a handful of ostrich feathers, and $800 T-shirts.

And also upstairs there's all this homewares stuff in the

Conran shop, which made me think I'll have to kill Camilla Parker Bowles and marry the Prince of Charles so I can buy some cashmere blankets and some sheer musliny jarmies.

But then I noticed I was the only person in the joint wearing Blundstones, and I got scared that one of the beefy security guards would ask me to leave – because there were all these very rich people milling around and I was thinking, 'Where are you people FROM?' I mean, there was a bloke in a bowler hat and a cape, and all these women who were wearing about $14,000 worth of clobber and looked like they went to the hairdresser every morning, and I was thinking, 'Where do you people go at night? I've never seen you before. I thought I knew this town!'

And there were all these roving bands of old ladies who were obviously loyal shoppers at the old George's store, which was just as posh and expensive but much more conservative, and they wandered around in little woollen hats, with brown stockings and string bags, going 'Where's the tartan section, Merle?' or 'Look out, Mavis, this G-string's a bit steep.'

The shop assistants were really nice and didn't once call me a peasant. And they were wearing these little charcoal-coloured cashmere twin-sets – for the fellas, a twin-set is a jumper and matching cardie over the top – and I just wanted to lay all the shop assistants down on those polished wooden floorboards and roll around in them. But I didn't.

I think it's probably also worth mentioning that I did get a bit of gossip out of the shop assistants, and it seems the

Conran shop mob flew this bloke out from England to dec-
orate the shop. And one of the things he did was put an
armchair under the stairs and surround it with neatly
placed potatoes – and I don't want to sound too patriotic,
but haven't we got an Australian who excels at a bit of armchair and potato work?

George's has since closed.

Bluey Billabong TV promo

[*kookaburra noises, other bird noises, sound of kangaroo jumping,
'Waltzing Matilda'*]

BLUEY BILLABONG [*wildly blokey Aussie voice*]:   G'day,
mates. It's Bluey Billabong here, invitin' yez to
watch m'new telly series, *White Bloke Wearing a
Hat in the Outback*. We'll show you the *real*
outback, where men are men and women are
generally horses. I'm a *real* Australian – that
means I can fly a plane, wrestle a croc, shake
down a shark, root a horse, drive a road train
and wear a French maid's uniform. Yeah, shut
up, Robbo, ya big hairy poof-dodger!

Check out the premiere of *White Bloke
Wearing a Hat in the Outback*. Fridee on
Channel 7, 8.30 p.m.

Crankypants: rug rats (continued)

You may recall me telling a little story the other day about a terrible house guest who came to stay at my house and ended up sitting on the couch in the nicky noo nar with my nanna's crocheted rug strategically positioned in the lunchbox region. I happened to pick up an American magazine recently – I *won't* name the magazine – and I'm not making this up: my rudey-nudey house guest has written an article about the decline of romance. It was a bit like reading an article by Boris Yeltsin on the decline of attractive dancing.

In this article my neurotic former house guest claims that a woman said to him in a 'delicious whispery voice', 'Call me. We'll play.' And then, I imagine, little baby piglets revved up and simply *flew* around his head in formation.

Ads again

[*New Age music, waves crashing*]

FIRST WOMAN [*breathy American accent*]:   Maternity eau de parfum. The new fragrance from Kelvin Klang for women who are up the duff. Maternity. If it smelled like anything at all, you'd probably throw up – again.

SECOND WOMAN [*whispering*]:   Maternity . . .

MAN [*deep, macho tones*]:   You want a sports drink that
you can hold upside down while it pours over your
head. You want a sports drink with a detachable
Swiss army knife. You want a sports drink that
can speak French and make your tea. You want
your head read, mate. Have a drink of water and
shut up.

Hatsh off to the
new millinerium (hic)

After a churlish Christmas message last week, it is encu-
cumber on this column to eluctable some of the fintobu-
lous events of the last year to remind us of rissoles to be
cheerful. Although I think I might be a bit hemmed over
from New Year's Eve during what, I may have had a few too
many money, I want m-u-u-uunny, that's what I want pah
doop a do, or I mayhem possibly dronken to excelsior.
Luckily I do not dronk and drab. My frock was absolutely
spectacles, as a mutter of fact.

Lists are uxorious in those circus stances, and so end of
years have magazines pocked with lists of mast splendof-
ulous scientific discovery of the century (never the hot-
water bottle always the bride, I mean computer) (and what
could passably come before contraception, certainly not
rotary hoe) (where was I?) and (b) most corruscatering
entertainer (dread heat between Acker Bilk and the Four
Kinsmen, lordy – apparently these lists are usually rotten
by old guys who go whoomph fainteroo if clap eyes once
upon a pierced eyebrow). (Note to editor: Where Aretha
Franklin? Where Dusty Springfield and Baby Spice? Où

est-ce c'est bloody bonjour Maurice Chevalier if it comes to that, sunshine?)

New Year's Eve is support-hosed to be a time of con-templatitudes. And it ish a time when columnists take the easy way out as above so nerny ner. Here is the frissons to be chief-full (good things from 1999 the year that was) and some predilictions furry new year channelled by Madame Inflamer, our poisonal middling. Personal medium. Shut up. Get some more champies, love, and bring mummy another ciggy. That's better.

Current events

- Finally we stopped aiding and abetting the Indonesian army and started aiding and abetting the East Timorese. Howzabout our troops, eh? Could we be

prouder? Not unless we'd knitted them ourselves.
Hurrah.

- General Wiranto's cabaret career nipped in bud.*
- Each Christmas message the Queen looks more and
  more like an Iced Vo Vo on legs, with a helmet. ('Love
  your neighbour as theyself,' said Mrs Windsor, who
  will no doubt sell Windsor Castle to help Glaswegian
  orphans.)
- We are soon to have a heroin-injecting room in the
  neighbourhood, which while not actually a beauty spot
  is far more charming a notion than the usual overdoses
  and syringes at the corner playground.

Album of the year
As Far As Life Goes by local gel Lisa Miller, featuring sing-
along classic 'Wipe the Floor with You' for anyone who has
had trouble with (1) love, (2) life, (3) Céline Dion.

Coolest couple
Forget Brad and Jennifer. We've got a couple of classy customers called the Deanes at Yarralumla. Instead of poncing
around the lawn talking about property prices with a few
penguined-up captains of industry, the Deanes invited some
junior transplant recipients to Admiralty House for New
Year's Eve to watch the fireworks.

---

*Has since released a CD. Damn.

Departures
Jeff Kennett. Hee hee hee.

Resolutions
I will never voluntarily wear a fluffy tiger-print Alice band.

Shoulder quaint ants be forgot and neeever something, something! O drunken cup of kind of thing, for the saaake of old lang's ine. For old lang's ine maffrin, for ol an zighn. Will drunken cup — oh, lordy. Oops! If you put salt on, it might lift the shtain.

Casino!

Episode six

[*fade up thrilling theme music*]

ANNOUNCER: Stay tuned for *Casino!*, the most
thrilling radio serial of the decade on *Foxy
Ladies*, sponsored by Lardypants Slimming
Studios! Coming up soon, it's *Casino!* Starring:

> **Jane Beagle** as Mrs Vernon Entwhistle the
> Third, a Duchess of Windsor look-alike
> **Dierdre Deirdre** as Binky Entwhistle, the
> heiress who doesn't know she's adopted
> **Davina Drizzle** as Pauline Spanky, the
> beautician with a heart of fool's gold
> **Richard Antelope** as the rich fool, Lord
> Ronald of Goat
> **Dame Leonie Puffdaddy** as Lorelei
> Watson the Third
> **and introducing –**
> **Fergus Hosiery** as Lefty Androgen, the
> gangster with a heart of lead!

Stay tuned for *Casino!*

[*theme music ends*]

ANNOUNCER: Last week on *Casino!* you heard Lorelei Watson say –

LORELEI WATSON: But, Miss Hack, if you have me thrown into that pit of rabid bison, I won't be able to sing!

ANNOUNCER: And now we cross to the casino beauty parlour.

LADY CHOOKY CRIPPS: Hello! Hello! Is that the casino beauty parlour?

PAULINE SPANKY: Yes, this is Pauline Spanky, the beautician. [*rustle of script*] Er . . . I don't think you're in this episode, Lady Chooky Cripps . . .

LADY CHOOKY: Balderdash, you heavenly idiot! I'm in every episode. I've got my agent sleeping with Judith Lucy. Now, I want to look like Katharine Hepburn by sundown. Can you do it?

PAULINE: Not without special effects.

LADY CHOOKY: Money is no object, you divine little squid. I've got gerzillions even if I am a little deaf and I misplaced a daughter in 1923. I've been reducing and I'm down to 375 pounds, if you don't count the bosom. I'll be leaving through your front door in a flash.

[*sound of phone being smashed to pieces*]

PAULINE: Yowser. And I've already got Michael Jackson in the Fading Suite and Julia Roberts in the Grin-stretcher. [*door opens and closes*] Oh hi, Mrs Entwhistle, you must be here for your appointment in the Exfoliating Pluckbuster?

MRS ENTWHISTLE: That's Mrs Vernon Entwhistle the Third to you, living proof that you can be too rich and too thin.

[*door opens and closes*]

LADY CHOOKY: Hello, you old trout!

MRS ENTWHISTLE: Well, I never!

LADY CHOOKY: That doesn't surprise me in the least, you prune-faced old praying mantis. Come out of the closet, Sir Ronald, I'd know that wheezing anywhere.

[*door opens and closes*]

COUNT RONALD: Well, I never!

LADY CHOOKY: Bollocks, I still have the photographs.

PAULINE: Lady Chooky, you're in with the impoverished but plucky Binky Entwhistle for a facial. Why, here's Binky now.

[*door opens and closes*]

BINKY ENTWHISTLE: Hello. Gosh, you look just like the only photo I have of my real mother . . .

[*door splinters into bits*]

LEFTY ANDROGEN: Don't anybody move! All you

dames can consider yourself – kidnapped!

[*everybody screams*]

ANNOUNCER: Tune in to the *Casino!* beauty parlour siege next week, when you'll hear the brutal gangster Lefty Androgen say –

LEFTY: Sister, I never thought of open pores as a problem before, but I'm beginning to see your angle!

[*music out*]

Dr Girly, I've misspelt my

lightning wand

Well, dear readers – not the weirdies who always spookily misspell things and never sign their names – this is my third-last column ever. (Oh, you know the type. 'Dear – not reely – So-called Msz Kooke, I can't stand people like you who always blame shop assistonts and men who have carports for the War. Why don't you stop writting about the rhodedendrons, so-called sexual harrasmont and [illegible green ink]. The End.')

It is, of course, difficult to restrain myself from writing about so-called rhodedendrons. But as predicted by Madame Inflamer, tantric wallet-lightener and seer, I'll be looking for a new job soon and so now it's time for this column to take final requests at kaz@token.com.au. The penultimate and final column subjects will be written to order.

To clear the decks, this week is a grab-bag of tit-bits I have been hoarding in a leopard-skin-print shoe box (in case Jackie Collins ever came over and asked to look at my ideas), presented here in no particular order.

1   Behold, a yellowing page from *In Style* magazine (or

it might have been *Greyhound Weekly*), in which several American celebrities are asked 'What's the most fabulous decorative gift you've received?' Lyn Sherr, an ABC News correspondent, said, 'I've written a book about giraffes, so people often give them to me. My favourite is a 20-foot-tall one that I keep on my back lawn.'

This was trumped by an author allegedly called Sugar Rautbord, with 'A Picasso that my ex-mother-in-law gave me. It's so decorative.' We can all relate to that. But lucky old Mary McFadden, a fashion designer, who got 'a pre-Columbian head'. Let's hope the embalming holds up.

2   Kutira Decosterd, a tantric-sex expert, was given her name, which means 'Temple of Love', by the Bhagwan

Shree Rajneesh, 'now called Osho', according to *Sex Tips: Advice from Women Around the World* by Jo-Anne Baker Kutira. Ms Decosterd is the founder of the Kahua Hawaiian Institute, which conducts Whale Adventures in Consciousness. (She's available for tantric weddings.) She believes that genitals are literally given a bad name, and she urges us all to adopt 'lingam', meaning lightning wand, and 'yoni', meaning crystal cave. Apparently 'Mr Helmet', 'funbags' and 'George W. Bush' are out of fashion.*

3   A woman surgeon (surely some mistake) has written to request a column on sexist things that have been said to her colleagues, such as 'I have four female surgical registrars at my hospital this year – and you know what? They're all different!' Sadly, no opportunities for a Robert Palmer video clip during rounds there. She also received a letter saying, 'In response to your request for a lower membership fee for your period of maternity leave, you will be classified as being overseas.'

4   It's easy to become mesmerised by the illustrations in *The Truth About Trout Flies* by the late Tony Sloane of Tasmania, including the Green Nymph, the Plastic Gum

---

*Any rude emails will be discarded by my beautiful assistant, Mr Mervyn Purvis, now head of costume wrangling at Token Artistes Pty Ltd. No lingam-related nonsense is ever passed on to affront my girlish gaze.

Beetle and the Modified Fur Fly. It is a follow-up to *The Truth About Trout* by his son Robert Sloane, the editor of *Fly Life* magazine. I imagine *The Truth About Trout Flies* to be a long-awaited exposé of the sort of nonsense the media has conspired to feed us about trout flies for years. It contains one of the best acknowledgements in Australian publishing: 'Lest I forget, to all those people who have assisted me through gifts of bits of wool, silk, cotton, feathers, dead birds, possum tails, rabbit skins and pieces of old fur coats.'

I plan to write to Princess Margaret requesting one of her old ocelot stoles. The thought of tying it onto a number 6 hook and chucking it in for a nibble is enough to keep me going for another week.

Review: *Men Are from Mars, Women Are from Venus – The Game*

We have had to add an extra answer for each of the questions in the actual board game as a reality check.

Questions for men
Most women would prefer to talk about:

a men
b shopping
c food
d Those aren't things we talk about, they're just things we do.

When a woman says, 'You're not listening', she means:

a 'I have something important to say'
b 'You used to listen'
c 'You're going to pay'

d She means all these things but, above all, she means you're not listening, which is why she formed a sentence with the words 'listening' and 'not' in them.

A woman who buys a man flowers is:

a sweet

b forward

c smart

d some kind of slut

A woman gets the most points with a man when she cooks:

a his favourite meal

b something new

c and cleans the dishes

d cleans the dishes, mows the lawn in the nude and works full time for his beer money

It's appropriate for a couple to make love:

a once they've made a commitment

b once they get married

c whenever the moment strikes them

d for example, at a parent–teacher interview, on public transport or on a card table during Christmas dinner with the relatives

You know your date does not want to kiss you, when she:

a avoids contact

b keeps moving around the room

c fails to remove the gum from her mouth

d throws up when she looks at you/hasn't turned up/goes
   'Euwwwwww' when you suggest it

Questions for women

The worst thing a man can be on a date is:

a arrogant

b cheap

c desperate

d dismembered

In bed, women generally want men to:

a talk more

b be spontaneous

c slow down

d stop snoring, farting and nicking the doona

If sex were a circus, men would be the:

a master of ceremonies

b lion tamers

c clowns in the small car

d assistants to the bearded lady

If my fantasy man were a horse, he'd be:

a a wild stallion

b a show horse

c a racehorse

d If your fantasy man were a horse, you'd be arrested.

Of the men I've slept with, I've been in love with:

a all of them

b most of them

c some of them

d Actually, of the men I've slept with, I've been introduced
   to all of them/many of them/at least one of them.

Ads again

[*New Age music, waves crashing*]

FIRST WOMAN [*breathy American accent*]:   Maternity.
     The new fragrance for pregnant women. Kelvin
     Klang's new eau de cologne for the foetus in you.
     Maternity. Like you, it's big, easily overwhelmed,
     and grumpy for no reason at all.

SECOND WOMAN [*whispering*]:   Maternity . . .

MAN [*deep, macho tones*]:   You want a sports drink that will
     satisfy you. You want a sports drink that feels good

in your hand. You want a sports drink that gets the newspaper in the morning and irons your shirts. You want a sports drink that can type, walk on a tightrope and negotiate peace in Zaire. Or you could just shut up.

Community radio dial twiddling

[*static*] G'day there. This is Rube Murchison on community radio 56.4 Gympie. Today we're going to play a Dean Martin song, but don't forget the Bowls Club ladies are down outside Safeway's selling preserves and unidentifiable knitted animals. Mmmmm. Marmalade. Buy a jar today and spread it thickly over a young man who — [*static*] Good afternoon. This is Stanley Went on community radio Bordertown 47 point oh oh seven. This afternoon we'll be talking to Bill Preston about mulching with grass clippings, Meryl from the pet shop will be popping in to help you with budgie mange, and Mr Petaluma Singh will have a crack at explaining the racial vilification laws during 'Russian for Beginners', right after the news. A two-wheeler bicycle was almost stolen outside the — [*static*] Hello there. This is Camberwell and district community radio station 67 point narn, and you're with Mrs Beverley Buttslammer. Before we hear a lovely song from a lovely man, a reminder that Jacqui and Jill's Antique Explosion is holding a sale of those lovely basins and jugs that people used to baaaathe in, back in the olden days. Nothing under $450. And, now, please enjoy William Shatner singing 'If I Were a Carpenter' — [*static*] Yeah, this is Geraldton community radio 94 point somethin', and yez all know me – Davo Davidson. There's a cattle duffin' meetin' up at the hall tonight, and ladies bring a plate, blokes bring somethin' to put on a plate, and in a mo' Slim Dusty singin' 'By Cripes the Tank Stand's Lookin' a Bit Rickety, Mum', but first the Ing-er-mar Bergman film appreciation mob will meet Tuesdee at — [*static*] Hi, this is Lorraine Slasher on community radio. That was an ace song called 'Really, Really Annoy Yer Parents' by Dead Pig Bits. We'd like to apologise for the incident at the community-radio-sponsored piercing festival last Thursday night in the shelter sheds on the median strip on Railway Parade. Would whoever has Melanie's school compass please return it before her maths exam on Tuesday. And now, it's 'Poke Your Tongue Out at Law and Order' by Pretty Damn Peeved — [*static*]

My nomination for the
Seven Wonders of Australia

My first thought was that in north-east Victoria there's those hills very close together that almost tell a story.

There's the Pimple, Mount Buggery, Mount Disappointment and Mount Misery. Was there more to Burke and
Wills than we've been told?

The obvious things to nominate for the Seven Wonders
are the kind of biggish ones: the Big Pineapple, the Big
Banana and, if you go on the Hume, the huge concrete
merino you see having sexual relations with a kiosk at a
Goulburn service station.

But I'd like to nominate the first of the pathetic big
things – there's a town in Tassie called Penguin with an
allegedly Big Penguin. It's about as big as Justin Madden.

I like to think that the townsfolk of Penguin operate like
penguins in the wild – where all the blokes stand on the
cliff, with the kids between their feet, while the mums go
out surfing, come home, vomit up some krill, and do it all
again the next day. And the town has given rise to some of
my favourite small-town signs: 'Penguin Mothers Club
meets here' and 'Penguin Recreational Centre'. I imagine
they juggle anchovies and play pool with polar bears.

None for the money, two more to go

As we swing into the second-last-ever column with the dextrous grace of a slightly shickered marmoset, I can only raise my slipper, filled to the brim with banana advocaaaaat, to you glorious readers who have responded so magnificently to request that one address certain matters before one is no longer available.

Although that letter from Juan Antoniou Pinochet Winterrranch is an obvious fake. That can't be how you spell Antonio, surely – we've all read *Woman's Day*. T. Mallon of Newcastle wants to know, seeing that he's so sure Wilson Tuckey is mad as a cut snake, 'Why can't I be sure about other things, like love and kindness and the value of education . . . and why do we eat chickens?' To which the answers are, they're smaller than us, Vitamin B12, and hey, yeah.

Dolly Adamson has emailed the diverting suggestion that I should keep my nipples to the wind, and when I find them I shall run them right up the flagpole. Rebecca Lister from Queensland wants to know whether anyone else is tiring of flash new cooking and getting out their mumsy

old cookbooks for 'whippings of eggs, butter, sugar, white flour and milk', as she so gorgeously put it.

Yes, Miss Rebecca. But seek ye the old-style recipes in new books such as Jill Dupleix's *Old Food* or Stephanie Alexander's *The Cook's Companion* (which can also double as a blunt instrument). In other words, Steamed Ginger Pud and Cusso yes, Mashed Ox Eye and Scattered Fowl Brains no.

V. Hatchet (a likely story) of Vermont writes to say he or she was OUTRAGED at seeing some firemen playing beach volleyball while their truck was parked up on the road. 'Your taxes at work,' the letter sneered. Yes, I'd much rather fire officers spent their shifts inside watching *More of the World's Most Alarming Buttocks* on video.

Heaven knows, if I'm trapped in a burning building, I don't want some fit bloke in the prime of his life coming in to get me straight from a vigorous volleyball game. No, *thank* you. If I've been overcome by a Hazchem cocktail on the thirty-fifth floor, send up a pasty-faced mattress-basher who smokes Holiday 60s, or Nick Cave. (For the record, the insurance industry pays for three-quarters of the fire service through a policy levy system, and local councils and the State government split the rest, which probably covers some shiny boots and a whistle.)

And in answer to those myriad inquiries about my future, keep your eyes on the bookshops until I find another job. As I have been standing on Mount Lofty in the nuddy waving a sign saying 'FREE KEG' for the last few days and so far have only received a request to dress up as Leaky the Incontinent Potaroo for a children's party in Doncaster, I wouldn't hold your breath. You may anticipate *The Little Book of Beauty* with 'Hints to Blokes' (sneak preview: Girls, if you're in a jam, why not use your G-string for a scrunchie? And chaps, it is best not to put your bum crack near the eye of a beholder), and my first children's book, *The Terrible Underpants*, will also be out later this year.

That's an outrageous plug, and why stop there? (What are they going to do, sack me again?) 'Where can I see Miss Judith Lucy?' asks Dottie Dicks, of Queanbeyan. You may come to Melbourne, Dot, to see her poignant, clever and too-funny-for-words show *Colour Me Judith*, at the Continental Café. BYO paper bag if laughing too much makes you hyperventilate. (Readers, if you have anything to plug, let us know BY TUESDAY, our risible deadline. Last chance for a school fete, for example, or perhaps the banking industry might like some flattery.)

Next week: the 'Banana Advocaat Song' ('And so, she's had a few, quite a few, certainly enough to mention'). (Alternative version, to the tune of the 'Banana Boat Song': 'Waay off, waa-aay off/Barman come and she missed-a the chair/Come, Mr Tallyman/Count up these glasses/Daylight come and she want a big rum'.)

Real readers' mail

Dear Ms Cooke,

Thank you for your spirited defence of firefighter fitness in your penultimate SMH column on Saturday 22 July. As with a vast number of your followers 'your' firefighters will miss your perceptive, humorous and clever writing. We hope you are never trapped in a burning building but if it ever happens your fit Firie readers would run the extra floor with a swifter stride to lift you to safety. We will miss your column.

Very Best Wishes for your next endeavours.

Yours sincerely,
Ian MacDougall,
Commissioner,
New South Wales Fire Brigades

In reply

Dear Commissioner MacDougall,

Well, you certainly know how to cockle the heart of a girl's warm tickles. Thank you, Commissioner, it means more than you know for you to take the time to send an email like that. Glad to be of service to the service.

(Not that I think it's in any way dignified to feed into those ridiculous fantasies that women have about being rescued by strong, fit men in a Firie uniform. But just say I AM in a jam and they DO run the extra floor, I don't suppose they could address me as 'little lady', could they?)

Incidentally, I am thrilled to be able to address someone as 'Commissioner'. It almost made me feel like Batgirl.

Maturely,
Kaz

Dear Kaz,

I read you are closing down soon. Before you go can you explain that flowery headdress and the loopy appearance in photo [see back cover].

Derek

In reply

Dear Derek,

For heaven's sake, man, that's a tiara and a sense of mystery.

Farewell,
Kaz

Review: *Bella's Blade*

You've got your contemporary erotic novels, in which somebody called Vanessa goes to Venice on a fashion shoot and is worn out by a bonking festival; or your historical romance, in which Mrs Slocombe goes whoopsie are those my bosoms again and is spanked by the king.

Today I am going to review Black Lace's book *Bella's Blade*, a historical erotic novel. Instead of a jaunty bounce on a haystack, we open with the heroine at the funeral of her – and I quote – 'deceased husband', she is being sexually harassed by her hideous brother-in-law, Oswald, and the whole shebang is set in the time of the plague.

On page 2 the author reveals in a jaunty aside that 'The gravediggers couldn't work fast enough to clear the backlog of diseased corpses, where death's stench filled the air.'

Two pages later Bella and a randy wimp called Anthony are tooling home in the carriage when they are confronted with 'the wasted corpses of victims being unceremoniously trundled away for mass burial'.

Getting aroused yet, anybody?

Soon Anthony is getting excited by the 'fruit-like swell of her white breasts above the scooped neckline of her funeral garb'.

And then 'He stripped off his braided red and black frock coat, his profusely buttoned long waistcoat and fiddly cravat, fumbling with the buttons of his ballooning white lawn shirt with its pin-tucked sleeves and frilled cuffs.'

I mean, the woman's obviously having sex with Elton John and that can't be right.

By page 44, where Bella has sex with a stranger on a coach, an escaped convict who was 'bearded, after several months without the luxury of a barber in prison, [and] stank like a compost heap'.

It's all tremendously erotic and I especially like the sweet-nothings dialogue on page 62 when Bella meets a Scotsman who announces 'Och, but ye make me ol' todger hard as an iron bar, lassie.' Sadly, Bella does not respond by saying 'It's so chumpy you could carve it.'

As usual, by the end of the book we've had it up to pussy's bow with serving wenches and blokes who keep whipping out their swords and sorting out some ruffians, Bella's had it off with the king, been kidnapped by foul-smelling pirates, been sold off in a slave auction, and by an amazing coincidence has a happy ending by meeting the smelly old convict she had sex with in the coach, who is, miraculously, Lord Flouncytrousers or somebody.

The *Foxy Ladies* rating? On the nose and not enough Mrs Slocombe.

Georgia Angelis, *Bella's Blade*, Black Lace, 1999. Recommended price $12.95 – take our advice: sort out your Tupperware cupboard instead.

Last ads

[*New Age music, waves crashing*]

FIRST WOMAN [*breathy American accent*]:   Maternity: Kelvin Klang has produced a new perfume for the pregnant woman. Maternity. It combines the scent of baby powder, fresh, fluffy towelling things – and lime-green poo. Get yourself in the mood.

SECOND WOMAN [*whispering*]:   Maternity . . .

MAN [*deep, macho tones*]:   You need a sports drink that's wet. You need a sports drink that comes in a bottle so it's not just a puddle in the shop. You need a sports drink with a top on it so it doesn't leak. You need a sports drink that doesn't taste like sump oil. And, just maybe, you need a sports drink that costs less than $4.50 a bottle. You need a drink of water. And a good lie down.

[*harp music*]

WOMAN: Hey, fatty, do you have a rather too
noticeable arse? We think so! Use Hoist-it Arse-
removing Cream morning and night and you'll be
amazed! Yes, Arse-removing Cream is the modern
way to a preposterous figure!

Grunge romance

BOFFO: Get us another beer, Shazza, you moll.

SHAZZA: Yeah, go and get rooted, Boffo.

BOFFO: I love yez, Shazza. Just coz I like shootin' up
heroin and battery acid and you're covered in
pustulent scabs, it doesn't mean we can't find
true love. Now, get us a beer or I'll boil yer cat.

ANNOUNCER: When a no-hoper loves a slag.
When Boffo meets Shazza. New from
Grunge Romance, an arresting novel called
Craven-A Sunset by Mildred Leviathan.
Because it's so much easier to spell 'love'
than 'co-dependency'.

ANASTASIA [*leaning closer to Craig's masculine scent and
dabbing at the vomit on his chin*]: You mean,
you're actually married, you have herpes and
a gambling problem? Why didn't you tell me?

CRAIG [*tossing fringe sheepishly and belching admiringly*]: I'm a selfish bastard and I wanted you to have sex with me.

ANASTASIA [*in a whisper, shuddering with joy*]: Thank you, darling.

ANNOUNCER: When a complete arsehole and a naive idiot meet. New from Grunge Romance, *Office Shemozzle* by Miffy Garden. Because it's so much easier to spell 'love' than 'psychotic episode'.

Farewell: parting is such sweet sherry

Obviously one would like to go out with a bang in one's last column, but you'd have to admit shooting JR's been done. Short of getting post-traumatic amnesia while appearing on a Ricki Lake show entitled 'Surprise! Your Boyfriend is a Cheating Swine, Yo, Actually a Real Swine with Hooves and All', I really couldn't be arsed.

Hence the plan to reflect some concerns of our readers. So, (a) may our anonymous, deafened and nerve-addled readers in Bega get a council vote against a local gun club; (b) if you have Lyme disease or want to know about ticks, send $5 for an info kit to PO Box 95, Mona Vale 1660; and (c) Shelley, the light aircraft pilot: no, don't take the kids up with you during school holidays – you'll be distracted, you'll say 'Go and play outside', and the next thing you know they'll be in *New Weekly* as stunt tots.

Letters (well, emails) have come from all around Australia, Maine, Dublin and a cruise ship anchored in Hong Kong Harbour. Thank you for your nutty and kind thoughts, and please excuse our inability to reply personally to everyone, as my undulatory assistant, Mervyn

Purvis, is the kind of overwrought party who is prone to drinking a bottle of sweet sherry with a crème de menthe chaser. And then just prone.

Oh, incidentally, team, you may have noticed last week that Western Mining Corporation head, Hugh Morgan, claimed, 'We've never done anything but seek to have the most proper and encouraging relationships with those who have traditional [Aboriginal] responsibilities.'

Right. Mr Morgan is indisputably an upstanding Christian member of the community, who would probably rather eat radioactive dirt than mislead us, so he must have forgotten that in 1991 he described a decision to protect an Aboriginal sacred site as 'neo-paganism' and opined, 'Ultimately, any religious nut, no matter how weird, can effectively expropriate property rights anywhere.' In 1984

Mr Morgan asked how land rights could be recognised if 'We cannot sanction infanticide, cannibalism and the cruel initiation rites which [Aborigines] regard either as customary or as a matter of religious obligation.'

Do feel free to insert your own extra adjectives (why not try a noun?) in the second sentence of the previous paragraph. I lost a few after a lawyer went through it like a man wearing mittens in the dark boning a fish. Honestly, do you reckon a columnist would ever resort to spelling out a message with the first letter of every paragraph? Of *course* I am not being sacked for feral sentences.

No, the newspaper you are reading is undergoing massive changes, in some cases redesigning whole pages, and this column is 'not required'. But one door closes and another one must be blown off its hinges using, say, Semtex.

Okay, so I would have liked to have been around to write during the Olympics. Firstly, so I could slag off the gymnastics training that reduces young women to stunted vessels of hope, and secondly so that while the eyes of the world are perving at Sydney, Donald Trump would notice me and whisk me (and any eggs nearby) to a secret location in Venezuela where I could train to host the Miss Universe pageant.

One must, before departing, apologise to all those senior students, several of them called Miriam, who have been forced to complete projects and write exam essays based on my work as 'satire', especially that question about 'What does Ms Cooke MEAN when she says . . .' Tell them

Miss Cooke says she's buggered if she knows.

Only a few more consonants to go before I stride out, alone, into the ex-columnist's wilderness with only Derryn Hinch, Shane Warne and someone called Bunty for company. Don't worry, I'd rather drink my own wee and then plummet to my death from a hidden mountain cranny than be seen with them. If I get a chance, I'll frag the lot of them with an exploding piñata full of pitiful payola. I raise, in tribute to you readers, a beaker of hospital daiquiri. *Hasta la vista*, babies.

Casino!

The final episode

[fade up usual theme music]

ANNOUNCER: Stay tuned for the final, thrilling episode in our long-running serial, *Casino!* Starring:

> **Pinky Halibut** as Lizzie Goody Good and Joan Hack
> **Francine Panto** as John Goody Good, Lady Chooky Cripps, Dash Trowel, Clive Strange and Lorelei Watson the Third **and introducing the Wally Furburger Orchestra.**

> Stay tuned for *Casino!*

[theme music ends]

ANNOUNCER: Last week on *Casino!* you heard Joan Hack say –

JOAN HACK: Hello, Lizzie, I haven't seen you around the casino much lately, you slack moll.

ANNOUNCER: And now on *Casino!* we hear Lizzie Goody Good reply –

LIZZIE GOODY GOOD: No, Joan, you miserable, desiccated old has-been – I've been away in Havana, where I shot Dash Trowel, Clive Strange, my husband, John Goody Good, AND his evil twin, Barry.

JOAN [*just being languidly polite*]: Oh. Dead?

LIZZIE [*distractedly, in the affirmative*]: Mmmm. Oh, hello, Lorelei. Care for a romp in the custard-wrestling salon?

LORELEI WATSON: Why, I'd sooner . . .

[*sound of something heavy falling: whistling noise, then splat*]

LORELEI: What was that?

JOAN: Just the casino share price, honey.

LADY CHOOKY CRIPPS: Hellooo, you marvellous little crustaceans, my corsetry and I were just orf to the roulette room when I heard that the *entire* casino has been set adrift from its moorings AGAIN, and we're going to hit ANOTHER giant iceberg! All hands on my bosoms!

JOAN: Frankly, Lady Chooky, I'd rather be gnawed to death by lethargic canaries.

[*sound of birds twittering*]

JOAN: Oh, my God, they're *coming* for me!

LADY CHOOKY: There's a first time for everything, Joan. Look out! The iceberg's got a gun!

[*general screaming, shooting, irrelevant sound effects such as train whistle, running feet, 'Advance Australia Fair', explosion, dying noises, very Goons*]

ANNOUNCER: Well, as discerning listeners will have noted, everybody is in fact completely dead, so that was the final episode of *Casino!* Next week, tune in to our spanking new cliffhanger drama, *Happy Deli*.

[*music out*]